Tackle

PERCY W. BLANDFORD

STANLEY PAUL
London

Stanley Paul & Co Ltd
3 Fitzroy Square, London W1

An imprint of the Hutchinson Publishing Group

London Melbourne Sydney Auckland
Wellington Johannesburg and agencies
throughout the world

First published 1961
Second impression 1963
Third impression April 1969
Fourth impression October 1973
Fifth impression April 1977
© Percy W. Blandford 1961

Printed in Great Britain by litho at The Anchor Press Ltd
and bound by Wm Brendon & Son Ltd
both of Tiptree, Essex

ISBN 0 09 096761 5

Tackle Canoeing

Contents

Illustrations

ILLUSTRATIONS

Between pages 48 and 49

8 Getting into a canoe from wading:
   (A) Hold the coaming well forward on each side, also grip paddle
   (B) Put one leg in well forward
   (C) Lower into seat, with hands brought back
   (D) Drop into seat and prepare to paddle, while bringing in other leg

9 Using a feathered paddle:
   (A) Arms are wide apart, left reaching well forward and right bent back
   (B) Left arm pulls blade back, while right goes forward with dipped wrist
   (C) Stroke is complete, then right wrist straightens as left blade comes out of water

10 The draw stroke to pull the canoe sideways

11 For sprint racing in a K1 the paddle enters the water at a steeper angle. The spooned blades are feathered and have assymetrical ends

12 Four canoes on a light trailer and two on the roof-rack are an easy load for a small car

Between pages 80 and 81

13 The hectic start of a long-distance race for young people

14 A typical easy rapid where the water is broken by falling over a shingle bar—on the Severn near Bewdley

15 A telemark turn:
   (A) The canoeist leans on to the paddle which is making a sculling stroke and turns the canoe on edge
   (B) From the other side the rockered effect presented to the water can be seen as the canoe tilts

LINE DRAWINGS IN TEXT

Foreword

A canoe represents the cheapest way of getting afloat, but that is not its only attraction. With it you can explore waterways ranging from little streams to rapid rivers and the open sea. It takes you away from the hustle of modern life, often without going far from centres of population. It opens up new holiday routes and, combined with camping, provides a unique and economical means of touring by water. Canoes may be transported cheaply and easily. A satisfactory canoe may be built by almost anyone.

This is a book on how to canoe—anywhere. It deals thoroughly with all aspects of canoeing as a sport and recreation. It is not a book on where to canoe, but brief details of some canoeing waters are given at the back of the book, together with sources of further information.

The author has canoed for thirty years and for much of that time has been fully engaged in canoeing and small-boat matters. He has absorbed a considerable amount of canoeing know-how, which he would like to share. This book represents what he feels to be the vital knowledge for a canoeist, but if any reader finds any query unanswered he will do his best to provide an answer if written to at BM/BOAT, London, W.C.1.

All the drawings and photographs in this book are by the author.

I

Modern Canoeing

CANOES have been developed in most parts of the world. In most cases they have been open. Only the Eskimo favoured a fully decked craft. Many canoes used by primitive people have been hollowed out from one piece, often by burning the interior away. In some cases the base of the canoe was hollowed from a log and further planking added to build up the sides. The Red Indians of North America made their canoes with birchbark skins, producing the predecessor of what is now generally called a 'Canadian' canoe. In Britain primitive craft developed in a slightly different way: coracles were made almost round, with a skin covering over a wattle framework. In Ireland the curragh was made by the same method, but more boat-shaped. These coracles and curraghs were the forerunners of much modern canoe constructional methods, although the shape is nearer some of the other primitive canoes.

Modern canoeing owes much to the various types developed by primitive peoples, but the birth of canoeing as we know it today is usually assumed to date from the canoe originated by John MacGregor, a London barrister, in 1865. He conceived the idea of a light boat, just big enough to carry himself, decked over except for a small well in which he sat, and propelled by a double-bladed paddle or a small sail.

He had this canoe built in traditional way, with clinker planking, but using cedar for a light construction, and he named it *Roy Roy* after his famous Scottish namesake.

With this canoe he toured British and then continental waters and wrote about his voyages. This fired the imagination of a great number of people and soon there were many canoeists using similar craft. The Canoe Club was formed in 1866. The Prince of Wales, later King Edward VII, was a canoeing enthusiast, and under his patronage the club became the Royal Canoe Club. The R.C.C. is still one of the leading canoe clubs, with its headquarters on the Thames a short distance above Teddington Lock.

Another early enthusiast was Warington Baden-Powell, the eldest brother of the Founder of the Scout Movement. He was particularly interested in sailing canoes, and was one of the pioneers in the development of specialist sailing canoes. By the turn of the century sailing canoes had become extremely fast—and expensive—sailing machines. Until the introduction in the 1950s of perfected catamarans, the sliding-seat sailing canoes were the fastest sailing machines afloat.

At the beginning of the twentieth century the sailing canoe was for the comparatively wealthy specialist, and ordinary canoeing slumped. Although it never died, there was no great enthusiasm, and little was published about it from before the 1914-18 war until the middle of the 1920s. Folding canoes were being developed in Germany. One story of the start of folding canoes concerns a German professor on a wet Sunday, who closed his umbrella as he went into a museum to pass the time, and saw an Eskimo kayak inside the entrance. He wondered if he could make a craft like that which folded in the same way as his umbrella.

From the earliest days there had been canvas canoes. In particular, the *Boy's Own Paper* published designs for this type of canoe. Canoeing in folding canoes ('faltboats') became an extremely popular activity in Germany in the 1920s. It spread and similar craft were manufactured in other countries, including England.

The Boy Scout Jamboree in Birkenhead in 1929 was attended by a contingent from Hungary which had a fleet of simple canvas canoes, which were used for a display, creating a considerable impression. As a result of this a design for the 'British Scout Kayak' was published in the scoutmaster's paper, *The Scouter*, and many thousands of canvas canoes must have been made from this design. By present-day standards this is a heavy and unwieldly craft, but it introduced very large numbers, including the author, to canoeing, and played a big part in launching canoeing as a sport and recreation.

From the 1930s onwards canoeing has made steady progress, with the development of both folding and rigid canoes. Home building has accounted for much of the increased interest. The interest has been mainly in general-purpose touring craft. Enthusiasm for straightforward racing has never been great in Britain although there have always been the devoted few. Entries have been made in the major international events, but without any outstanding successes. However, progress is being made, but the opposition from countries where racing is tackled much more seriously is considerable.

After the Second World War canoeing has become extremely popular—at first possibly because it provided a cheap way of getting afloat when supplies were short. It benefited by the general boating boom of the 1950s. The popularity of slalom as a spectacle did much to show canoeing to the public and to educate them in its technique, largely through the medium of television in the first instance. It has brought about a change in nomenclature. The word 'canoe' at one time conjured up a picture of the open Red Indian craft, and the decked kayak type was rather an unknown quantity to the general public. Now the word 'canoe' is taken to mean a decked craft propelled by double-bladed paddles, without any further qualification to the name.

Slalom has also brought about great improvements in general technique. Much of the technique was already known in a limited way, but now the technique of the average canoeist is far better than it was, due to the influence of the expert white-water men. The need for the ability to make the canoe do exactly what was wanted, and avoid penalties or gain valuable seconds, has caused the slalom enthusiast to search for strokes and techniques. He has learned many from Canadian canoeing and from Eskimo kayak work. All of this has added up to a general improvement in canoeing standards.

Another post-war development has been the organization of courses. At one time, five minutes instruction was considered enough to let a new canoeist loose on placid water, and he learned the rest by experience. Now the job is tackled much more systematically, and the beginner, if he wishes, can be trained in building and using his craft, enabling him to become a proficient canoeist in a much shorter time than might otherwise be the case if he had to depend on trial and error. In particular, the Central Council of Physical Recreation have played a big part in the organization of courses. Canoeing is also practised as a school activity, and this development has introduced large numbers to the sport and recreation.

Another development of the 1950s has been long-distance racing—using courses of many miles involving natural hazards. Straightforward racing has received some encouragement by the organization of sponsored regattas, usually in association with rowing. Canoe touring continues to be the backbone of the activity as a recreation. Organized tours have become increasingly popular; both parties arranged for those with some experience and their own canoes, and trips arranged by travel organizations who provide all equipment for beginners.

Organized canoeing

Canoeing appeals to many because of its freedom and independence, but even the most go-as-you-please canoeist will benefit by joining a club. He will share in the accumulated knowledge and maybe contribute something to the

1. A plywood canoe is light. There is a moulded seat and the cockpit coaming takes the spray cover which the canoeist is wearing. He is also using a British Standards Institute approved lifejacket.

2. The same canoe afloat. This canoeist is wearing a buoyancy aid and has the spray cover fitted. She is leaning forward and about to dip the paddle blade as far as she can reach, close to the canoe, to start a long powerful stroke.

3. A canoe will take you where no other craft can go—these are
on a sunny river of southern France

4. Part of the framework of a folding canoe, with one end assembled, showing the tensioning arrangement of the bottom

5. A spray cover with elastic around waist and coaming

6. A single-seat canoe is most conveniently carried over one shoulder

7. Getting into a canoe from the bank:
(A) One foot central and hand on coaming
(B) Weight is transferred to the canoe, with a steadying hand on the bank
(C) Use hand on coaming to lower into seat, then stretch legs

common cause. With his support the organizations may be able to speak for all canoeists and obtain results only possible with the backing of numbers. All canoeists benefit by the actions of those who serve the sport and recreation as representatives of organizations.

The international body controlling canoeing as a sport is the International Canoe Federation. Representatives of national bodies meet periodically and are responsible for the organization and control of all forms of racing and competition internationally. Apart from the organization of races, they draw up specifications for craft.

The national body controlling canoeing as a sport in Britain is the British Canoe Union. This is a federation of most of the canoe clubs of the country. There is a separate Scottish Canoe Association, but this is affiliated to the B.C.U. and operates as part of it. The British Canoe Union looks after the interests of canoeing in Britain as well as representing it internationally. The B.C.U. is responsible for national championships and national competitions, although the organization of events is usually deputed to clubs. All matters of canoeing interest are the concern of the B.C.U.—they can provide home and foreign touring information, they publish books and pamphlets, have a film library, conduct tests and appoint coaches, watch the legal rights of canoeists, and co-operate with other bodies of allied interests.

Most keen canoeists find it worthwhile joining the British Canoe Union as well as a club, so as to obtain maximum benefits and support the bodies looking after canoeing interests. Britain has more canoe clubs than any other country. Many of them are small and the majority serve only their immediate locality, but where a nearby club exists that is the one most likely to be of value to any canoeist. Local knowledge added to that available through the B.C.U. can be of considerable service to the enquiring canoeist.

The Canoe-Camping Club differs from other member

clubs in the British Canoe Union, in being a large national one. It is a section of the Camping Club of Great Britain and Ireland, and membership of the C.C.C. includes membership of the Camping Club as well as of the B.C.U. As most canoeists are also campers, this brings them many useful benefits including books, magazines and camp-site information. Where no local canoe club exists, individual canoeists find C.C.C. membership worth while, and many value C.C.C. membership as well as that of a local club.

2

Canoe Types

ALL double-ended craft propelled by paddles may be known by the general name of 'canoe'. At one time there was a tendency to keep the word mainly for what is now termed a 'Canadian canoe'—the open Red Indian type of craft, usually propelled by a single-bladed paddle. Rigid decked craft, propelled by double-bladed paddles, were loosely termed 'kayaks'. At the same time, folding versions of these craft were, rather inconsistently, called 'folding canoes'. This nomenclature is still favoured in America, but elsewhere mention of a 'canoe' is assumed to mean a decked craft, and this is qualified as 'Canadian' if an open canoe is intended. The word 'kayak' (or any of its many alternative spellings) now means a craft modelled on the lines of a Greenland or Eskimo kayak, or a racing craft; which may be designated 'K1', 'K2' or 'K4', the number indicating the number of its crew. 'Foldboat' is sometimes used as the name for a folding canoe, being the translation of the German 'faltboat'.

Sizes
Experience has produced sizes which are generally accepted, particularly for general-purpose touring craft, of the rigid or folding decked type. The smallest single-seater is 11 ft. long and about 28 in. beam. This will carry an adult and a reasonable amount of kit, but it cannot be very fast and there will be a tendency to yaw. Anything shorter will yaw excessively, i.e. the bow will swing from side to side

with each paddle stroke. On an 11 ft. length the slight
amount of yawing may be tolerated for the sake of economy
in size and price, but it is better to have a longer canoe.

The general-purpose single-seat touring canoe most
favoured is 14 ft to 15 ft. long and about 26 in. beam. This
is more roomy and considerably faster—or easier to paddle,
which is the same thing. It is possible to compromise, with
a length of 13 ft. and a beam of 27 in., and this is a popular
size for young people.

The sporty two-seater tourer is 17 ft. long and about

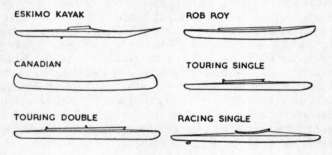

FIG. 1

Typical canoe profiles

32 in. beam. This has considerable carrying capacity as well
as being fast. Rigid canoes of this size are not so popular,
because of their bulk for transport, and 15 ft. by 30 in. is
more common. This will take two adults and their lightweight camping kit, but packing is more of a problem than
with a single-seater or the larger two-seater.

In a 17 ft. two-seater the feet of the rear paddler come
behind the front person's seat. In a 15 ft. two-seater they
come each side of the seat. Although a shorter canoe may
carry the weight of two people it is not advised as they come
closer together and may interfere with each other. The front
seat comes almost between the knees of the rear paddler,
and when he makes a powerful long stroke he may hit the

head of the man in front. Unless timing is perfect, the two paddles may clash occasionally. The length may be brought down to 14 ft. for two young people, but that is the absolute minimum advised.

Speed is related to length, so racing canoes are made as long as possible. Great length brings directional stability, i.e. the tendency to keep going in the same direction. If this becomes excessive the canoe cannot be turned, even with a rudder. Consequently racing canoes are a compromise between the desire for maximum speed and the need for manœuvrability. For straightforward racing the limiting sizes permitted by the International Canoe Federation rules are as given in Chapter 7.

For sea work only a canoe may be much longer—a single-seater 17 ft. or more long is easier to keep on its course in a confused sea, and with plenty of space its rather larger turning circle does not matter. Its speed, or ease of propulsion, is valuable in the strenuous conditions which may be met. A foot-operated rudder is usual for sea canoeing so that more of the paddling effort may be kept for propulsion.

For canoeing in broken water, shooting rapids and slalom competitions, the canoes are better for a greater degree of manœuvrability than is desirable for placid water or sea canoeing. In some slalom canoes this is taken to the extreme where the canoe is so directionally unstable that it is almost impossible to keep it on a course if an attempt is made to tour in it.

A few enthusiasts favour a modern version of the Eskimo or Greenland kayak. This differs from normal touring canoes in being longer and narrower, with a swept-up stem and a very small cockpit. The Eskimo did not work to measurements; as his aim was the chasing of seals he needed all the speed he could get, consequently his craft was up-ward of 17 ft. long and under 20 in. beam. Modern versions are built in the conventional rigid and folding way, instead of sealskin over a driftwood framework. In skilled hands a modern Greenland kayak is a fast seaworthy canoe, but experience is necessary and this is not the craft for the lone beginner. Of course, it is the ideal craft for doing an Eskimo roll—in fact mastery of this is almost essential to the Eskimo kayak paddler, as he will need the technique for the same reason as the Eskimo, to keep upright.

Unlike the Eskimo, the North American Indian wanted carrying capacity rather than speed, so his canoe has always been beamy. The modern Canadian canoe follows this trend and the general-purpose canoe is quite full in its sections. Popular sizes in the U.S.A. are between 15 ft. and 18 ft. long and between 33 in. and 36 in. beam. Canadian canoes made in Europe tend to be narrower, and therefore faster but less stable. All methods of rigid construction are used. Although there have been sectional Canadian canoes, the author has never met a folding one.

Characteristics

Manœuvrability in a rapid river canoe is obtained by making it shorter than a touring canoe and by giving the keel a 'rocker'. In side view the keel line of most touring canoes is flat. A rockered keel is swept up towards the ends. This is also done to aid turning in the long racing canoe. Excessive rocker means that part of the keel is above the water, and speed is little better than a canoe of that shorter waterline length. In the best designs the rocker should finish at or just below the actual waterline at the ends when the canoe is stationary.

One way of trying to get the lines of a longer canoe is to cut off the stern so that there is a small transom. The lines then are drawn as if they were continuing, to meet perhaps 2 ft. aft of the actual stern. This is of doubtful advantage, and it is debatable whether a craft with a transom qualifies for the name 'canoe'. If the transom comes much below the surface there will be drag due to the disturbed water left abruptly astern. If it is wholly above the water the value of the extended lines is lost, but there is the advantage of a broader bottom to the craft right aft, minimizing the tendency to suck down at high speeds.

Stability in a canoe depends on the height of the seat of the paddler and on the cross-sectional design of the canoe. A reasonable height of seat is advisable for ease of paddling, allowing longer and more powerful strokes than when the seat is low and the arms have to be lifted higher. However, the height has to be considered in relation to the form of the hull cross-sections.

A broad flat area around the central part of the bottom gives the maximum initial stability. A cross-section which is absolutely flat gives maximum stability (Fig. 2A). However, this will not produce very efficient lines and will pound in waves. Skin friction is reduced to the minimum if a hull form with the minimum wetted area is used. This has a semi-circular cross-section and very little stability (Fig. 2B). Despite its lack of stability, this form is found in racing canoes, where speed is of first importance. A more usual rounded cross-section has the centre of the semi-circle flattened to look like a 'D' on edge (Fig. 2C). With a reason-

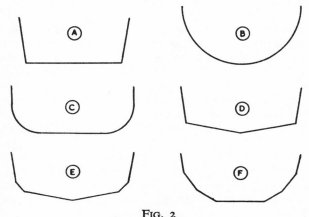

FIG. 2
Typical canoe sections

ably flattish area around the middle of the canoe this has ample stability and lends itself to the production of good lines, and is the accepted shape for round-bottomed touring canoes.

The best hull form has rounded sections and the only reason justified for other sections is the limitations of materials. When plywood sheets are used the hull has to be designed to allow for the fact that, except to a very limited degree, they cannot take a compound curve. If the inefficient flat bottom is to be avoided, the section is given a V and the shape is known as 'hard chine' (Fig. 2D). The chine is the angle between the bottom and the sides. A closer approximation to the round bottom may be obtained by having double chines (Fig. 2E). Fabric-covered folding and rigid canoes are approximately round-bottomed, but because of the widely spaced lengthwise members the section is more correctly multi-chine (Fig. 2F).

Because it is double-ended, a canoe is very nearly symmetrical below the waterline, and canoes are built with the same sections each end. However, it is more usual to have the greatest beam slightly aft of amidships, allowing the crew to come aft of the centre, which is better for steering. Having fuller lines aft also does something to counteract the tendency for the stern to pull down into the water when the canoe is paddled hard. Having the greatest beam forward of amidships gives a shape more like the streamline of the aircraft wing, or the shape of a fish. Moving the centre of buoyancy forward means that the crew have to be moved forward and there is much more stern deck than foredeck. This hull form can be faster, but it is difficult to steer by paddling and a rudder has to be used. The important shape is that which is immersed. It is possible to give exaggerated shape to the gunwale line, while the waterline is near normal. Considerable flare has been given to the forward sections of rapid-river canoes to make them more buoyant after dropping into a trough or over a fall, but most whitewater canoeists favour normal lines. Tumblehome (having the greatest beam lower than the gunwales) can make paddling easier, as the gunwales are not as wide, but it has not found favour. Carried to excess it reduces stability if the canoe rolls.

Some light sailing craft and many motor boats will plane—lift partly out of the water. The hull has to be designed for this with a broad flattish run aft. The idea has been tried on a canoe—a deep V forward running into a fairly flat bottom aft. Although a powerful paddler can just about get the canoe on to a plane, he is not strong enough to keep it there, so the greater speed which comes from the great reduction of skin friction cannot be obtained.

Constructional forms

Canoes may be rigid, folding or semi-folding. Rigid canoes are most popular, as they are simple and cheap, and not as big a transport problem as might be supposed (see Chapter 4). Folding canoes dismantle to pack into two or three bags. Other types have been made which fold in width or depth, without reducing the length; or which are sectional, possibly with the dismantled parts nesting.

A rigid canoe is always ready for use and does not involve the canoeist in work at the beginning and end of a trip. A folding canoe takes about twenty minutes to assemble or dismantle. Its skin has to be dried out after use. The framework assembles in the skin with tensioning arrangements (Plate 1) so that the finished canoe is comparable with a rigid canoe. A packed folding canoe usually goes into a large rucksack and another bag perhaps 4 ft by 1 ft. diameter. For home-building, a rigid fabric-covered canoe is much simpler and cheaper. Some professionally made folding canoes are examples of fine craftsmanship.

Most rigid canoes are fabric-covered, but they may be plywood, or moulded in veneers or glassfibre (see Chapter 9). Early canoes were built with clinker or carvel planking (Fig. 3). Modern laminated methods were anticipated a century ago with shellac and paper over a mould.

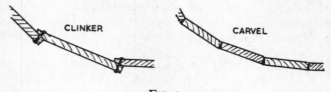

FIG. 3
Sections of planked hulls

Semi-folding canoes have been made with solid bottoms attached to semi-rigid decking by canvas sides held tensioned by struts, which could be released for folding. Another type has rigid wooden sides, with canvas bottom and decking. The sides are sprung apart and held by frames, giving a hard-chine form. Sectional canoes may be made with each part independently buoyant, clipped or bolted together. It is possible to have a single-seater in which the pointed end sections nest in the cockpit. It is possible to use rubber in compression to make watertight joints between parts which are not separately watertight. In any form of sectioning there can be a considerable strain on the fastenings, and this type of building has never proved completely successful.

Paddles

McGregor started canoeing with a double-bladed paddle made from two oars. Blade area was soon increased; the accepted size for a general-purpose touring paddle is now about 8 ft. long, with a maximum blade width of 7 in. and an effective length of 15 in. A central joint simplifies packing and allows twisting. The whole paddle may be solid wood, or the blades may be laminated.

Solid paddles are usually of spruce with the blade built-up (Fig. 4A). Lightness in a paddle is important. Some makers favour a built-up blade (Fig. 4B). Thin strips of mahogany, or other contrasting wood, may be glued in the joints (Fig. 4C). It is possible to lighten the paddle by

26

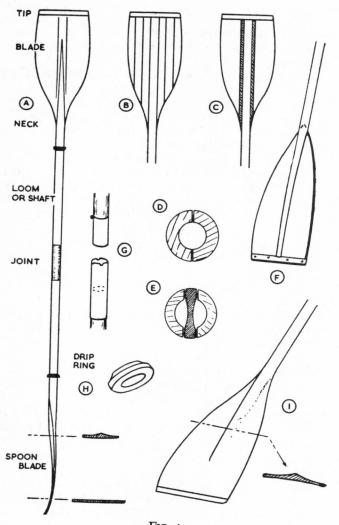

TIP

BLADE

(A)

NECK

(B)

(C)

LOOM
OR SHAFT

(G)

(D)

JOINT

(E)

(F)

DRIP
RING

(H)

(I)

SPOON
BLADE

FIG. 4
Paddle details

hollowing the looms (Fig. 4D). Because of possible weakening when doing this, strips of mahogany may be built in (Fig. 4E).

The loom of a paddle with laminated blades extends for most of the blade length and is curved to suit (Fig. 4F). Although it is possible to spring thin plywood to shape the best blades are built up of veneers glued in a mould. The tips of all blades should be protected with thin copper or salt-water-resistant alloy riveted on.

The telescopic centre joint should have a locating screw and notches to engage with it (Fig. 4G), so that the blades may be parallel or at right angles in either direction. Drip rings (Fig. 4H) are intended to break the flow of water running down the loom from the upgoing blade.

A spoon blade with a central ridge is traditional. It is probably more effective if the ridge is on the back, and racing paddles are made this way (Fig. 4I).

Paddles have been made considerably longer than 8 ft., but variations today are more often in reduction of length. In theory the closer the blade works to the side of the canoe the less will be the turning effect and the greater the propulsive effect. The shape of the canoe limits the shortness of the paddle. The narrow racing canoe may have a paddle about 7 ft. long, but in a touring canoe anything much less than 8 ft. is difficult to use.

A slalom canoe is low and slightly narrower than most touring canoes. In it it is necessary to make a variety of strokes quickly. The sport is hard on the paddles and there are many breakages. A rather basic pattern with straight blades is often used. All-metal types have been used.

Spooned paddles are difficult to make without special tools, but laminated blades may be made at home, or straight-bladed solid paddles are possible with ordinary tools (Fig. 5A).

Single-bladed paddles may be made in the same way, with

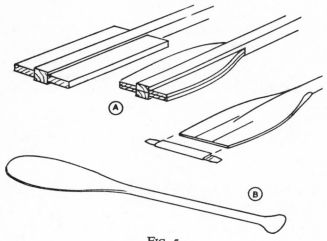

FIG. 5
Paddle construction

built-up blades and grips. For correct use in a Canadian canoe the paddle should reach from the ground to about eye level. The top should have a comfortable grip (Fig. 5B).

Seating
Paddling is easier and more efficient if the seat is as high as the stability of the canoe will permit. A rigid seat is better than temporary padding. Simplest is a sloping box top (Fig. 6A). Better is one shaped fore and aft (Fig. 6B). Better still is one moulded from Perspex or glassfibre. A backrest is not essential for propulsion, but for comfort in touring it is advisable. A fixed backrest (Fig. 6C) or a strip on the coaming (Fig. 6D) is not as comfortable as one which is located at the top of the hip bones and allowed to pivot (Fig. 6E).

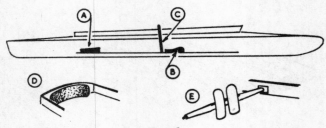

FIG. 6
Seats and backrests

Spray covers

In anything but settled weather and placid waters a spray cover is advisable, which keeps water out but does not prevent the canoeist getting out in an emergency. In a small-cockpit single-seater the spray cover may be worn by the canoeist, with elastic around the waist and coaming (Fig. 7A and Plate 2). Another type forms an overall cover, held

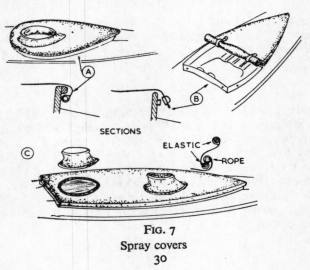

SECTIONS

ELASTIC
ROPE

FIG. 7
Spray covers

by press studs and rolled forward to make a breakwater when in use (Fig. 7B). In a combination of the two types, the canoeist wears a piece which is held by elastic to a large opening in the main cover (Fig. 7C). In emergency only the skirt comes away with the canoeist.

Painters

A canoe is rarely moored as it is simpler to lift it out, but ropes on the ends are used for several purposes. The best attachment on a rigid canoe is a brass strip (Fig. 8A) to

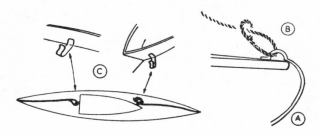

FIG. 8
Painters

which the rope is eye-spliced. (Fig. 8B). On some folding canoes the painter fastening is sewn on, but it is better if it goes through the skin to the framework.

The painter should be rope not more than $\frac{3}{4}$ in. circumference. A bow painter longer than the canoe and a short one on the stern will serve most purposes. Painters stretched along the side decks from end to end provide something to grab in the event of a capsize. Hooks on the coaming will hold the painters ready for use (Fig. 8C).

Canoeists' knots are few. The common bend (Fig. 9A) is the correct joining knot. The reef knot (Fig. 9B) is only correct if it bears against something. A round turn and two half-hitches (Fig. 9C) is better than a clove hitch (Fig. 9D)

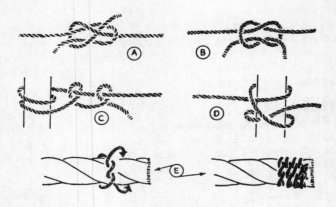

FIG. 9
Basic knots

for fastening the end of a rope to a post or ring. Rope ends should be whipped with thread. A simple strong whipping is the West Country (Fig. 9E).

Other accessories

It is easy for an enthusiast to overburden his canoe with gadgets. The value of a particular accessory should be weighed up before accepting it. A paddle bracket is a near

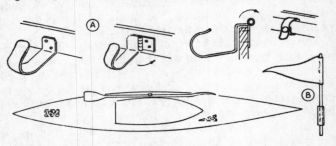

FIG. 10
Paddle brackets and flags

essential (Fig. 10A). Flags are best sewn on the deck. If a staff is used, a section of rubber tubing (Fig. 10B) will prevent the wood breaking off. A club pennant should be used forward. If you want to show your nationality have a Red Ensign aft.

3

Basic Technique

PRACTICAL canoe handling is best learned in two stages. The first stage is comparatively short and is soon mastered, and some people get all they want out of canoeing without going far into the second stage, which consists of dealing with broken water.

A beginner can go afloat and soon make the canoe do what he wants. At this stage it is easy to adopt wrong methods, and it is inadvisable to rush ahead without learning from the experience of others, either in personal instruction or by reading about technique.

Launching

It is easier to damage a canoe ashore than afloat, so more care is needed when launching and lifting out. It is wisest to adopt a rule that canoes are always lifted and never slid along the ground. To launch a canoe single-handed, lift by the coaming at the point of balance, steadying against the thigh, then put over the bank stern first (Plate 3). Lower the stern into the water and move the hands towards the point of the cockpit, while the water takes the weight of the other end. Transfer the hold to the gunwales and then to the stem and lift the canoe in.

Two people launch by holding opposite sides of the coaming and lifting it in a generally similar way. By using these methods the canoe is passed into the water without rubbing the bank. Although it is possible to launch a narrow single-seater sideways over a low straight landing stage, it is better to regard endwise lifting as the normal routine. When launching stern-first any current will cause the canoe to swing bow-upstream, the correct direction to start in running water.

Remove a canoe from the water by a method the reverse of launching. After disembarking, swing the canoe bow-on to the bank and lift the end clear of the water, until it can be lifted near the point of balance. If there has to be a pause during launching or lifting out, the canoe may be put down partly over the edge.

Launching into shallow water at the edge of a river or on the coast needs care to ensure that the canoe will still be afloat when the paddler is on board.

A canoe with its crew seated is surprisingly stable and seaworthy. Trouble comes when standing or crouching, as one must at some point when embarking or disembark-ing. Remember to get the weight low as soon as possible. To avoid disconcerting wobbles, work centrally—one foot behind the other rather than side by side. Take the weight on one leg, and never share the weight between the canoe and the bank. Do not kick out when getting in or out.

There are two methods of embarking, depending on whether it is being done from a bank or from wading in the water. Entering from wading is simplest, while it gets progressively more difficult as the bank gets higher.

Entering from a low bank is probably the commonest circumstance (Plate 4). Face forward and put the nearest foot in centrally and well forward of the seat. At the same time grasp the coaming with the hand on the same side as the foot. In a short cockpit hold the point of the cockpit, other-wise hold well forward on the side away from the bank. Hold the bank with the other hand, but do not lean on it. Have the weight directly over the foot in the canoe. Put the other foot behind it and lower yourself into the seat. If you have to adjust your position after sitting, put both hands on the sides of the coaming, not on the bank.

Getting on to a bank from a single-seater is the reverse of

embarking. Position the feet and pull your weight over them, or push up on the coamings at the sides of the seat. Hold the bank and step out without kicking. Never turn parallel to the bank—you should be facing forward until clear of the canoe.

To get in from wading alongside the canoe (Plate 5), face forward and hold the far side of the coaming opposite the seat. Lift the near leg into the cockpit far enough forward to allow you to sit down, but keep your weight over the leg in the water. Move your body over the cockpit and at the same time put the other hand on the near side of the coaming behind you, so that both hands are ready to support you as you take your foot off the bottom. Drop into the seat. There is no immediate hurry to bring in the other foot—you can drain water from it first.

Getting in from deep water is not advised. Getting in from surf is liable to be wet. The canoe should be at right angles to the waves. If it is possible to stand astride the canoe and drop in that will be easier than the normal way of getting in from wading. It is better to find shelter. When landing in surf the canoe should be kept end-on, then a wave may take you high and dry.

What to do with the paddle is not always obvious. If there is a paddle bracket, it may be there. It may be better to hold it in one hand. In placid conditions it may rest across the cockpit. It is not good practice to leave it on the bank, where you may not be able to reach it.

When getting in from a bank level with the canoe it is possible to put the paddle across the back of the cockpit so that it rests on the bank and steadies the canoe as you lean on it while entering. This is particularly useful for the close-fitting Eskimo kayak.

Getting in from a high bank is basically the same as getting in from a low bank, but as the weight is kept higher for a longer period it is more important to avoid sharing the weight between the bank and canoe, and to keep the load central at all stages.

With a two-seater methods are similar, except that

normally one holds while the other moves. With the greater stability there is a temptation to take risks, and use unsatisfactory methods which would lead to trouble in a single-seater. When wading in running water the canoe must be held longest at the upstream end—the forward person gets in first, and the aft paddler gets out first. Similarly, coming alongside in a flow of water, the canoe is turned upstream and the bowman holds the bank while his mate gets out and goes to hold near the stem.

Stance

A beginner will soon find that he can control his craft in placid water after very little practice, but he will see the expert apparently getting much more for the same amount of effort, and his control is much more precise. The difference is experience.

The position in the canoe affects the stroke. The pull of the blade is transferred to forward motion only through the body. The main contact is the seat, but there are the feet and often the knees. The back does not count as the pull is away from the backrest. Firm contact is essential to efficiency. Air cushions and foam rubber may increase comfort, but there is a slight loss of efficiency due to them making weak links in the propulsive chain. A thick wobbly seat might be hazardous, due to it allowing the body to move independently of the canoe.

A moulded seat gives a greater area of contact and is therefore more comfortable. Paddling is easier from a high seat, but the limit is governed by stability. The thighs should be level with the top of the coaming in most touring canoes. A seat may be 3 in. high in some single-seaters and up to 5 in. in some two-seaters. A footrest is worth having. It may be a simple crossbar (Fig. 11A) or a raised piece. A hinged board (Fig. 11B) supports the whole foot. The touring canoeist may brace his knees under or against the coaming when he wants extra power, but the slalomist makes grips (Fig. 11C).

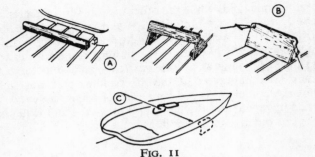

FIG. 11

Footrests and knee-grips

Ordinary paddling

To the newcomer it seems natural to use a double-bladed paddle with the blades in line with each other. However, most enthusiasts favour having the blades at right angles to each other. In fact, this is quite a natural way to handle the paddle and it feathers the blade in the air, reducing wind resistance, which is quite a consideration in a head wind. With a spoon-bladed paddle it is possible to twist the blades at right angles in two directions, and a locating screw and notches should be arranged in the joint to allow for this (Fig. 4G).

The paddle should be held so that the hands are a little farther apart than the width of the shoulders. A racer holds close to the blades, but this is tiring for touring. A common beginner's fault is to bring the hands closer together and make short strokes as he gets tired.

Paddling must be done with both arms—it is not just a matter of pulling on one side. The other arm must thrust forward until almost straight. This uses the power of both arms and makes the stroke as long as is comfortably possible. The stroke can be made even longer by swinging the body towards the side of the immersed blade, but this is tiring and it is not usual to move the body much at the waist when touring.

38

The blade should only just be immersed, and the shaft held at an angle that just clears the coaming. Lifting too high is a common beginner's fault. Paddling speed depends on the paddler, but the beginner tends to use rather short ineffective fast strokes, when he would get more for the effort if he used long slower strokes.

The use of the twisted, or feathered, paddle may be practised ashore. Twisting is done with one hand. The loom is allowed to twist in the other hand. If a firm grip is held there, there is an unnatural downward bend when pushing forward. Which hand is preferred for twisting will have to be found by experiment. If twisting with the left hand is adopted the paddle should be arranged so that when the left blade is pulling the spoon of the other is upwards. If the blades are straight and may be used either side, the same twist will do in both cases.

To make a stroke with a left-handed twist (Plate 6), hold the blade normally with the left hand and make a stroke (Fig. 12A). Pull through for the length of the stroke and thrust forward with the right hand. Lift the blade out of the water. While both blades are in the air, dip the left wrist so that the blade comes horizontal and the right blade becomes vertical ready to enter the water (Fig. 12B). Hold the shaft loosely in the right hand as the left wrist is dipped. Keep the

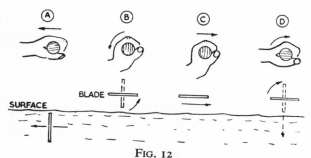

FIG. 12
Feathering a paddle blade

left wrist dipped, tighten the grip of the right hand and make a stroke with the right blade, keeping the left wrist dipped the same amount throughout the thrust forward (Fig. 12C). Lift the right blade out of the water and straighten the left wrist (Fig. 12D). You are then ready for the next stroke on the left side and the sequence is repeated.

When twisting is first used afloat, strokes should be weak and slow. Two main faults, likely to need correcting, are twisting while the blade is still immersed and using the blade at an angle other than a right angle to the surface of the water.

Steering is done by varying the power applied each side. The art of steering is in applying correction before the canoe has gone far off its course. The beginner tends to let the bow go too far, then over-correct. Later, steering becomes instinctive.

If the canoe has to be turned more, strokes may be given on one side only. For a tighter turn strokes are made forward on one side and backwards on the other.

A canoe has no brakes. To stop a canoe quickly the paddle should be used on both sides with short sharp backwatering strokes. If the canoe has a fair amount of forward way on it care should be taken to brace against the first shock of reverse paddling. The first few strokes will be little more than holding water. With spooned blades it is not usual to reverse the blades for backwatering.

Coming alongside a bank needs practice. It is too easy to either hit the bank or find you finish too far away. Every boat pivots on a point and in a canoe this is well forward—probably near the point of the cockpit. To bring a canoe alongside it should be turned into the current, or the wind if that is stronger. When the bow is almost at the bank, either paddle harder on the bank side or backwater on the other side (Fig. 13). Arrive slowly.

In a two-seater all that has been said about single-seaters applies. Two paddlers working together can outstrip a single-seater, but until they are used to each other

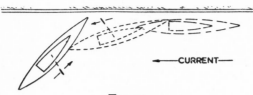

FIG. 13
Coming alongside

much effort will be wasted. The paddler in the stern has
most effect on turning. Because he has control of the canoe
he must be skipper. The only exception is a racing canoe
where the forward man may be steering with a foot tiller.
In a tourer the front man keeps up a steady stroke unless he
is asked for special action.

The stern man paddles in time with his mate and keeps on
course by pulling harder one side or the other without
losing time. Where necessary he asks his mate to pull harder
on one side. For a sharper turn both may paddle one side
only. For a turn on the spot one paddles forward on one side
and the other backwards on the opposite side.

When shooting rapids in a two-seater it is usually best for
the forward man to hold his paddle across and high enough
to miss waves, while his mate paddles through. He can give
an occasional stroke, but in broken water it is most important that decisions are only made by one man. Similarly,
when coming alongside, it is best for the decisions to be
made by the stern man only.

Special paddle strokes
For most of the time the average canoeist only needs to
understand straightforward paddling, but there are a few
simple strokes worth mastering. The Canadian canoeist has
always been proud of his variety of strokes, and the double-
bladed paddler is finding that some of this single-bladed
technique is adaptable to his needs. Of course, in narrow

41

waters, half a double paddle may be used as a single paddle.

The canoe may be moved sideways by a draw stroke. The paddle blade is parallel to the side of the canoe, immersed well out from it and pulled in (Fig. 14A). To get the most effective leverage the hand is held close down to the blade (Plate 7). With a single-bladed paddle it is possible to turn the blade and slice back edgewise to make the next stroke, but with the spooned blade it is wiser to return out of the water.

Opposite to the draw is the push-over. Instead of pulling, the canoe is pushed. The paddle starts near vertical, close to

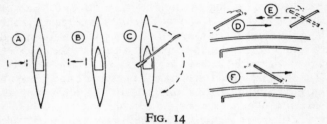

FIG. 14
Special paddling strokes

the side of the canoe and the lower arm thrusts out at the same time as the upper one pulls back (Fig. 14B). Both draw and push-over may be done diagonally when the desired movement is other than a right angle.

It is usual to turn sharply by paddling forward one side and back on the other, but there is an alternative worth knowing. This is a sweep. The hands may be in the normal position, or the stroke is more effective if the paddle is extended more on the side being used. The blade is held vertically, well ahead and swept in an arc of almost 180 deg. (Fig. 14C). Starting at the stern it becomes a reverse sweep, but the normal sweep is usually more effective.

Sculling has many uses. The principle is that of the man in a dinghy, who propels it with an oar over the stern, worked from side to side. A blade pulled normally through the water produces a reaction at right angles to it. If sliced through edgewise the propulsive effort is negligible. If pulled at an angle midway between these two the reaction can be resolved into a component thrusting against the boat and another at right angles to it. If the action is made alternately in opposite directions the crosswise reactions cancel out, leaving only the forward thrust on the boat.

Sculling may be included with the draw stroke. The paddle is held at a steep angle, with the lower hand at the top of the blade and the other well up the loom. Only about half the blade is immersed (Fig. 14D). The blade is moved parallel with the side of the canoe at an angle to its direction of movement, alternately backwards and forwards (Fig. 14E), pulling with the lower arm and thrusting with the upper one. The effect is a smoother move sideways than with a simple draw stroke.

In a sculling draw stroke the leading edge of the paddle when moving is farthest from the side of the canoe. If the nearest edge leads it becomes a push-over sculling stroke and the canoe moves the other way (Fig. 14F).

Another use of the sculling stroke is to prevent a capsize or correct a partial one. It is also used in one method of rolling. If the paddle is extended well out one side and sculled backwards and forwards on the surface, it has a good resistance to sinking and may be leaned on with considerable pressure. As a test it is possible to grip the canoe with the legs and lean progressively farther until the side decks are awash (Plate 8).

Clothing

Safety should be thought of as well as protection when choosing clothing for canoeing. Safety precautions are described in Chapter 5. Clothing which might seem ideal for bad weather when ashore might be dangerous in an accident afloat.

In general the usual outdoor dress of shirt and shorts makes a satisfactory dress for canoeing. Wading should be accepted as normal, and bare legs regarded as usual. Only on rare occasions, such as canoeing briefly from a landing stage in cold weather, should stockings be worn. Because of their danger in a capsize rubber boots of any sort should not be worn.

Plimsols make satisfactory footwear, particularly if holes are cut to allow water to drain out. Sandals may be better, but leather is unsuitable, due to hardening, and fabric shrinks. Plastic sandals are probably best, except that some have bottoms which collect mud. There should be something to protect the big toe against stubbing on rocks.

Shorts should be short and lightweight. Corduroy and leather get dangerously heavy when wet.

Probably the ideal wet-weather canoeing clothing has not yet been discovered. Anoraks are most popular. If they are loose-skirted they will go outside the spray cover. Anything which keeps rain out keeps perspiration in, so fully waterproof garments should not be worn more than necessary. A porous cloth, such as gabardine, will keep out rain for some time, without causing excessive perspiration. This type of garment may be worn for warmth when it is not raining. A garment made from plastic sheeting is fully waterproof and does not stretch. Within its limitations it is cheap and satisfactory. Heavy anoraks and similar jackets should be avoided.

In cold weather the lower half of the body is protected in the canoe and the upper half is kept warm by movement and there is no need to wear thick clothing. However, a sweater should be ready to put on when you go ashore.

Canoeing is an activity which invites people to wear less than they might elsewhere. After a day in the company of scantily clad canoeists it is easy to forget that what you regard as normal may not be approved elsewhere. Canoeists going ashore should check that what they are wearing (or not wearing) will not be an embarassment in the place they are visiting. A reasonably dressed man, or preferably woman, is much more likely to get the desired response when approaching a farmer for a camp-site!

4

Canoe Touring

MOST people use their canoes mainly for touring, either day trips or extended cruises. The lightness and portability of a canoe makes exploration of all kinds of water possible. Obstructions to other craft may be portaged and the canoe may be transported overland to remote waters. It will float in water too shallow for other craft. It will carry sufficient kit for its crew to be almost completely independent of other people. It is possible to link up waterways by short overland trips. A canoe brings exploration within the reach of its crew. Even a place which is well known from a shore approach takes on a new look when it is approached from the water for the first time, and the canoeist appreciates something of the feelings which an explorer has when he first sets foot on new territory.

Canoe touring does not need any elaborate preparations, but the canoeist should *always* find out his rights on the waters he intends exploring, and he should learn from experience of others what he can hope to accomplish and what equipment he should have. Every canoeist, whatever his ultimate specialization, should gain experience in touring. To go from place to place, fully equipped and independent of others except for the purchase of stores, on peaceful waterways making a complete contrast with the crowded roads, and not being bound by timetables or even the need to fill up with petrol—in these hectic days this is a complete change and the ideal holiday.

Fortunately there are thousands of miles of waterways in

the British Isles which the canoeist may use, but it is wrong to assume a right, and every canoeist should have some knowledge of the legal position, and should make enquiries about a waterway before going on it. In general there is a public right of way on tidal water. Elsewhere the water is private, unless a public right of way has been established.

A canoe may be used around the coast and as far up estuaries and inlets as the tide reaches, without asking permission or paying a fee. How far the tide reaches up some estuaries, particularly those of the low East Coast, is difficult to define. Fees are demanded, for instance, on the Norfolk Broads, although there is a slight tidal effect. On other rivers a weir and lock more clearly define the limit. Teddington, on the Thames, is an example. Estuaries are probably controlled by a Harbour Board, or other authority, which may make regulations, but these do not usually affect canoeists. The Harbourmaster is the man to consult if you have any doubts.

The right to use water, whether tidal or not, does not automatically include overland access to it. You must find a public landing place or obtain permission from the landowner. Legally, the foreshore is private above high water mark. You may land anywhere between high and low water marks, but you may not be permitted to go above high water mark. This is a point to watch on many islands in tidal waters, where the owners insist on their seclusion.

Where the water is non-tidal, in law ownership of the land surrounding the water includes ownership of the bed of the river, and you have no more right to go over the river-bed because it has water on it than to go over the private land. In practice there are a great many owners who do not object to canoeing, and there are other exceptions detailed later, but the point should be remembered. If you go on a private river you are trespassing, in the same way as if you walked on private land.

Where there are different owners of opposite banks, the river is assumed to be divided down the middle. Non-tidal lakes and lochs are treated in the same way legally, and it should not be assumed that because a lake is large it is necessarily free to use.

Public rights of way on many rivers have been established in the same way that rights have been established on footpaths over private ground. In most cases this means that use of the water is free and permission need not be obtained. The legal right of way may be for only part of a river. In many cases the owners of the right on other parts may not object, but the actual limits should be checked. The Severn is a right of way for almost the whole of its length. The popular Wye is a right of way from Hay to the sea, but in fact no one objects to canoeists starting a few miles higher at Glasbury, although, because of fishing, owners are not so tolerant higher than that. The Shakespeare Avon is a right of way only downriver of Stratford.

The largest English lake—Windermere—is a public right of way and so is the largest British lake—Loch Lomond. Most other lakes of the Lake District are private.

On some rivers where a right of way has been established work has been done to improve navigation. On such rivers as the Trent and the Severn there are a few locks where an inclusive fee is charged for locks and navigational river. The Thames, upriver of Teddington, is an example of a river with a right of way, yet a fee is charged by the Thames Conservancy Board, De Bohun Road, Reading, Berkshire, which manages it, for the use of the water as well as for the locks.

On a great many rivers where there is no legal right of way the owners have never objected to canoeists. On a few rivers there are parts where canoeing is not permitted, although for the greater part of their length it is. Use by occasional canoeists is rather different from large organized parties, and care should be taken in organizing club or other official events to avoid using waters where there is any doubt. Obtaining permission from a series of landowners may be difficult, if not impossible.

Canals are man-made navigable waterways. In Britain most of them were made in a hurry in the middle of the nineteenth century as business concerns. The coming of the railways took much of the expected traffic and few of them have ever made a profit, but today they must be considered as business concerns, even if unprofitable ones. Consequently, the canoeist is a customer who has to pay. Fees are demanded and must be paid before a canoe is put on a canal. There are several methods of payment, with reductions for clubs and other organizations, but in general canoeing on canals is not cheap.

Most British canals are controlled by the British Waterways Board. Licences to use the canals are obtained from Pleasure Craft Licensing Office, Willow Grange, Church Road, Watford, Herts. For administration the country is divided roughly north and south and east and west through a point near Birmingham into four areas, each with its own office, from which information may be obtained.

Besides the canals the British Waterways Board is responsible for the navigable sections of certain rivers which connect with canals, notably the Trent and the Severn. A canal licence covers use of these rivers as well, although there are river licences at lower rates for those who do not wish to use the canals. On canals most of the locks have to be worked by those taking craft through, but on the rivers there are staff to work the locks. Lock fees on most waterways are becoming incorporated in the licence fees.

For the few canals which are not controlled by British Waterways Board, there are offices at the canals where licences may be obtained. One useful short connecting canal, that is controlled by the National Trust, is the Stratford-upon-Avon Canal, linking the Midland canals with the Avon at Stratford.

Because of the large number of locks, many canals are hard work, but some, such as the Llangollen Canal, are worth canoeing for their own beauty. Where a canal

8. Getting into a canoe from wading:
(A) Hold the coaming well forward on each side, also grip paddle
(B) Put one leg in well forward
(C) Lower into seat, with hands brought back
(D) Drop into seat and prepare to paddle, while bringing in other leg

9. Using a feathered paddle:
(A) Arms are wide apart, left reaching well forward and right bent back
(B) Left arm pulls blade back, while right goes forward with dipped wrist
(C) Stroke is complete, then right wrist straightens as left blade comes out of water

10. The draw stroke, to pull the canoe sideways

11. For sprint racing in a KI the paddle enters the water at a steeper angle. The spooned blades are feathered and have assymetrical ends

12 Four canoes on a light trailer and two on the roof-rack are an easy load for a small car

incorporates part of a river, or links lochs, such as the Caledonian Canal, it is usually attractive. On some very busy commercial canals, canoes, and sometimes all other pleasure craft, are prohibited or restricted to certain times.

The relationship between canoeists and anglers is more a matter of mutual tolerance and goodwill than one of law. The angler is paying, sometimes heavily, for his sport, while the canoeist often pays nothing. Where there is a right of way or the canoeist is paying or has permission, the angler has no legal right to expect any special treatment from the canoeists, whatever he may do out of common decency.

When the canoeist is on water where exception has not been taken to canoeing although there is no legal right, his relations with irate anglers calls for some diplomacy. In general the right to fish from a bank, which is all that most individuals and clubs rent from a landowner, does not give them any right to control boating. However, if they protest to the owner, who is drawing a fee from them, he may prohibit boating—which he has a right to do.

On the better fishing rivers anglers pay considerable sums for fishing rights. Naturally, a man paying hundreds of pounds for the fishing rights of a short stretch of salmon river will not welcome a canoeist who crashes through without permission. The higher reaches of many rapid rivers are carefully preserved for fishing and should be avoided by canoeists. On some it is possible to obtain permission outside the fishing season.

The average fisherman is a reasonable fellow, and if we behave reasonably and respect his wishes and beliefs we shall have done all we can to maintain good relations with him, and he is likely to reciprocate.

Pass fishermen so as to cause the least interference. Drifting by on the far side of the river will be understood as an attempt to cause the least disturbance. Keep outside the casting area. If the fisherman is wading it is better to pass behind him. Call to him to let him know that you are coming, if he has not seen you. If there are several of you,

keep together and go in single file, so as to cause the least
disturbance for the briefest time. Be polite. A fisherman and
a canoeist glaring dumbly at each other do not make for
good relations.

Being in a canoe does not absolve the canoeist-angler
from the need for a permit to fish. The same applies to
shooting, and the best advice to the touring canoeist is to
leave gun and rod at home.

Information on the legal position of various waterways is
best obtained from the British Canoe Union. The British
Canoe Union *Guide to the Waterways* is a comprehensive
book which is also available to non-members.

Abroad the position is generally simpler. Canoeing on
most continental rivers is without restriction and free.
Obviously, advance information should be obtained, but
there are usually no formalities to bother about. The travel
secretaries of the British Canoe Union have up-to-date information on most rivers in which there is any canoeing
interest.

Canoe-camping

The majority of touring canoeists camp—the two go together.
The camper who comes to canoeing will be pleased to find
that he has more stowage space in the average canoe than
he has in rucksack or saddlebag. Canoeists' camp kit is much
the same as for other branches of lightweight camping.
Obviously, there is no room for bulky patrol tents and
large cooking pots. Two-man tents are usual and cooking
is done on stoves.

The art in packing a canoe is to break the load down into
small packages. The best containers for bedding and clothing are fully waterproof bags, made of rubberized fabric
with strips stuck over the seams. A long narrow bag is
preferable to a short thick one. The neck should be sealed,
either with cramping pieces of wood held by wing nuts and
bolts, or by tying, then doubling back and tying again.

Fabric-backed plastic may be used for bags, but unbacked

plastic does not stand up to pushing through frames for long. If cheap polythene bags are used they should be enclosed in cloth bags.

All items should be stowed so that they cannot fall out. Articles in the vicinity of the cockpit should be tied in. What to do with valuables is a personal problem. Some money, at least, might be carried on the person in a belt with a built-in purse, even if other money is packed with clothing in a waterproof bag. A non-waterproof watch may be sealed in a transparent bag. With photographic equipment you must weigh up the need for protecting the gear against the need to have it available for use.

Weight in a canoe does not make a great difference to the effort needed to propel the canoe. If there are many portages weight must be considered, but otherwise items which might be thought luxuries may be included.

In camp the canoe stands beside the tent and acts as a store tent. Painters may become clothes lines or guylines. Buoyancy bags may form pillows.

Kit stowage should be practised. There is plenty of room in a touring single-seater, but careful packing is more important in a two-seater. The trim of the canoe must be considered. The high foredeck invites the packing of more kit forward, but not too much weight should be put there without compensating weight aft. If a canoe is down by the bow it is difficult to control. It is better to be slightly down by the stern. Kit should not be stowed where it would impede getting in and out. Some items which may be needed during the day may go at the sides of the seat.

Canoe-touring parties

A canoe-camping trip with one or two canoes is enjoyable, but a trip with a large party has many attractions, particularly where all are members of a club or organization, or where beginners want to learn how to canoe under an expert leader, or are tackling a river more advanced than they feel capable of doing without expert guidance.

A trip with small numbers may be undertaken on most waters without much advance preparation, but with large numbers catering must be planned ahead, and this means fixing camp-sites in advance. It is usually best to camp at the start, so that preparations may be made leisurely and thoroughly.

The length of daily stages is difficult to determine, as there are so many variable factors: visits ashore, the number of hazards, the experience of the members, the flow of the river and the camp-sites available. A basic figure for a party is fifteen miles per day, made up of five hours paddling at three m.p.h. If there are locks you may be delayed about twenty minutes at each of them (Plate 10). A helpful current can add to the daily distance, but if there are frequent rapids—even trivial ones—the party will be delayed as each canoe shoots in turn. On a canal locks are usually portaged and it may be the number of locks and not miles which count in assessing a day's stage.

There is no need for every day's stage to be the same distance. Usually, the location of suitable camp-sites may make differences of several miles. If there is a place worth visiting ashore the daily distance may be shortened to allow for it. There may be two nights at one site to allow for visiting and relaxation, possibly with a regatta in the evening.

If all members of the party are experts there need be little organization, but it is best to make a rule that no canoe should ever be out of sight of others, so that help is available in an emergency. If the party are beginners or even expert young people, the leader is morally, and possibly legally, responsible for the safety of the party. He must take all reasonable precautions and know what he would do in any possible contingency. Every member should be able to swim a reasonable distance and be briefed on what to do if capsized (see Chapter 5). Canoes should have buoyancy bags, and in really hazardous waters lifejackets should be worn.

The most canoes that one person should be responsible for is about ten. A larger party should be divided with sub-leaders. Someone should be detailed as the last one in each group, so that if the leader sees him he knows the whole party is present. With a large party and many groups, there are several experts at the head of the convoy and a repair team at the rear. If a hazard is reached where guidance is necessary, an expert stays there and directs the groups through. What guidance is needed depends on the experience of the members. If the experts are comparatively few, one group may be pilot patrol for the day and travel with the leaders, so that a member may be briefed on a hazard and left to direct the groups through.

Members of a group must keep together, but groups need not keep within sight of each other. If a canoe is damaged its crew are helped ashore and left with basic repair materials to start repairs while waiting for the repair team. Each group should also have basic first-aid equipment, but is it a help if someone in the party has more comprehensive gear, and can be responsible also for latrines and disposal of rubbish; the actual work being done by the duty group for the day.

Catering is a job to be done before the start of the trip. Certain basic things may be ordered at the start to last for a few days. Things should be ordered at each site for eating there and at the midday stop next day.

The ideal staff will be made up of the leader, his assistant, a caterer, a first-aider, two or more repair men and a bosun, who is the leader's runner, whose major job is rousing the camp in the morning. Besides these jobs the staff should all be expert canoeists.

It is best to attempt to get a reasonable part of the day's distance covered in the morning. If the camp is roused at 7 a.m. a start may be made about 10 a.m. after a good breakfast. There should be a break of about an hour for a light snack midday, then the next site is reached about 5 p.m. and a large meal prepared in the evening.

Transport

Canoes may be carried short distances by one or two persons. To lift single-handed hold across the coamings near the point of balance and rest the hull against the thighs as it comes up. It may be carried a short distance in this way. but it is better to move up to the shoulder under one coaming for a greater distance. If two people are available the canoe may be carried by its ends.

A canoe loaded with camping kit should be carried by four people to avoid strain on the canoe—one at each end and one each side. Canadian canoes are portaged inverted over the head and for a long single-handed carry a decked canoe may be managed in this way.

For transporting more than a short distance, most canoeists prefer a trolley, consisting of two light wheels on a folding framework, which straps to the canoe, about one-quarter of the length in from one end, so that it is wheeled from the other end.

A canoe on its trolley may be towed behind a bicycle, either fastened behind the saddle or from an extension bar. The law does not permit a canoe to be towed behind a powered two-wheel vehicle, although it is permitted behind a three or four-wheeled vehicle (including a motor-cycle combination), providing the trailer itself is attached to the towing vehicle and complies with certain regulations about springing, lighting, number-plate, etc. However, most car owners prefer to carry on the roof.

The curve of the coaming of many canoes conforms closely to the curve of the roof of many cars. The inverted canoe may rest on a blanket and be lashed directly on the roof. It is better to have a roof-rack. The best type consists of two separate assemblies with simple crossbars at the top. The type with projections for carrying ladders is not so suitable. One or two canoes may be carried the right way up on the crossbars and lashed down to the bars. Two more canoes may be inverted on them, reversed so that the points of the cockpits come inside the backs of the coamings.

If more than four canoes are to be carried, a trailer will be needed. Light dinghy trailers may be adapted by fitting crossbars (Plate 9). Four canoes may be put on this in the same way as on a roof-rack, then a fifth put centrally on top. Special trailers are available where the canoes fit into racks.

Folding canoes are easier to transport by car. Some pack small enough to go in the boot, but the long bag in most cases will have to go on a roof-rack. With any type of canoe, paddles need extra care in packing.

Any type of canoe may be transported by rail. Folding canoes of normal weight may be taken as baggage at no charge on British Railways. A rigid canoe may be taken by rail at excess luggage rates providing it can be got into the luggage van. In practice, on British Railways, the limit of size for getting into most vans is 13 ft. However, a rigid canoe of any size may be sent at 'passenger-parcels rate'. The charge is by weight (not size) and distance.

5

Watermanship

ANYONE who goes afloat and tackles boating seriously acquires a sense related to the new medium in which he is enjoying his activity. This teaches him to treat water with respect, knowing what he can do and what he cannot. He learns to read conditions from the appearance of the water. This extra sense is something which cannot be learned from a book, but if he has the urge to become a fully competent seaman or waterman, there is much he can learn from the experience of others, which will help him to more quickly do the right thing by instinct and avoid the trouble which the uninitiated may invite.

Reading water conditions is dealt with elsewhere in this book, but the waterman acts on these signs in a safe way. If he doubts his ability to deal with the conditions he takes appropriate precautions. At all times he knows what he would do in emergency. He has anticipated all likely contingencies and planned accordingly. If he takes risks they will be calculated ones, and he knows what he will do if the worst happens. He does not get himself into trouble which will involve people other than those with him into inconvenience and he does not wilfully cause them to accept danger on his behalf.

That does not mean that the good waterman is ultra-cautious. He still enjoys himself, but if he gets his fun out of taking risks he appreciates what he is tackling and understands the consequences of things not going according to plan—which is very different from being reckless.

Buoyancy

The first thing that the good waterman thinks of is the sea-worthiness of his craft. Apart from choosing a canoe which suits the conditions he expects, he is concerned that it will remain afloat under all circumstances. All normal canoes should be perfectly watertight. If your canoe leaks you should attend to it.

A capsized canoe traps air under the decks, and even a badly holed canoe usually holds air somewhere, but what would happen in the event of complete waterlogging should be considered in relation to each particular canoe. An empty rigid canoe with a painted canvas skin would almost certainly float awash. It would with a light plastic skin, but with a stouter plastic or a rubberized fabric skin, it would probably not have enough inherent buoyancy to remain on the surface. A folding canoe, with its metalwork and heavy rubberized skin, would not remain afloat. A canoe with a wooden skin, either solid wood or plywood, should float a little higher than a painted canvas one. Metal or glassfibre construction has no buoyancy in the material, so a canoe completely waterlogged would sink.

Apart from the desire to save the canoe, there is the need to consider the crew in the water. The canoe should have sufficient buoyancy to support them. The higher it floats the easier it will be to salvage. The worst is most unlikely to happen, but the prudent canoeist gives his canoe a reserve of buoyancy in case it does.

Special buoyancy bags are made to fit in the ends of the canoe. They are triangular and may have long tubes which reach the cockpit and allow inflating or topping-up while in position. This is advisable, as an inflated bag may not go through a frame. One of these each end of a fabric-covered or wooden canoe will provide enough buoyancy for a waterlogged canoe to float quite high and support a good weight. The standard bags should be sufficient to prevent all but the largest glassfibre or metal canoes from sinking.

There are several alternatives to the standard bags.

Football bladders are often used. They do not contain as much air as the triangular bags, but they seem adequate. Tubular inflatable lifebelts, obtained cheaply through surplus sources, are sufficient. A car or motor-cycle tube is more than enough, but it occupies too much room if kit is to be carried.

There are several solid buoyant materials, usually expanded rubber or plastic foam. These are particularly suitable for building in glassfibre or wood canoes. Pieces of the material may be located in the extreme ends or under decks where they will not take up valuable space. Air bags are more usual for flexible-skinned craft.

It is possible to build in air compartments during plywood or glassfibre construction. A foot or more at each end may be completely blanked off by a bulkhead, or frame without an opening. A drain point with a plug should be provided. Occasional withdrawal of the plug and confirmation that the inside is still dry makes for your peace of mind. Apart from any doubt about the compartment still being effective, the built-in buoyant compartment seems to take up more stowage space than an air bag, which can be pushed into shape to a limited extent to permit the stowage of gear. The obvious bulging of an inflated bag is a comforting sight in bad conditions. Some makers have carried the business of building in buoyancy to extremes, with almost the whole of each end sealed off, making the stowage of kit and even the stretching of legs impossible.

Buoyancy when fully loaded with camping kit is not such a problem as might be expected. Waterproof bags of kit contain a surprising amount of air—which is all extra reserve buoyancy, providing the bags are jammed or tied in. It is not usual to increase the size of air bags when carrying kit.

Another type of air bag sold by canoe maufacturers is long and tubular and intended for fastening along the gunwales. Two bags are used, each at least as long as the cockpit and 3 in. or more in diameter, held to loops on the canoe skin at intervals. The effect is to increase the beam at gunwale level, so that if the boat rolls, the buoyant bag rests on the water and prevents the canoe going farther. They are useful when using a high sailing rig, but for paddling, most canoeists regard them as an impediment to the use of the paddles and a certain amount of drag on their progress. Some folding canoes have inflatable gunwale air bags which are inside and tension the skin during assembly. These do not obstruct paddling, although this type of canoe is rather beamier than normal.

A paddle which goes adrift in an accident is a nuisance. Attaching it to the canoe by a light line from its centre to the point of the cockpit has been advocated, but not many canoeists do this.

Personal buoyancy

Whether to wear a lifejacket or not is something which each canoeist will have to settle for himself. It is not just a question of the ability to swim well, as will be seen when we discuss capsizing. In an emergency there may be several things to do, such as fending off rocks or branches, gathering loose gear and controlling the canoe. A lifejacket relieves the wearer of the need to think about swimming as well as the other things he may have to do. In placid waters or even mildly rapid rivers most canoeists would not bother with a lifejacket, but on the wilder rivers or at sea the enthusiast realizes the common sense of personal buoyancy and wears a lifejacket. For many events, such as slaloms and open sea races, the organizers state that lifejackets must be worn.

The best lifejacket for a canoeist has probably not yet been invented. There are some excellent jackets intended for other forms of boating, but many of them have drawbacks when considered in relation to canoeing. The yachtsman and dinghy sailor do not have to do the regular arm movements of the canoeist, and many of their lifesaving garments cause too much obstruction to be satisfactory in a canoe.

There has been considerable research into lifejacket design and the results can be rather confusing to the newcomer who wants safety in a device which will not impede his movements, particularly his paddling action. Unfortunately, buoyancy cannot be provided without bulk somewhere. There are many lifejackets made to a British Standard Specification, which will float an unconscious person on his back with his mouth above the water. Other jackets are more properly called 'buoyancy aids' and are considered sufficient to support a conscious person who wants to retrieve gear or right a boat. These are made to a standard set by the Ship & Boat Builders National Federation. Other lifejackets are made to a British Canoe Union standard and are similar in major respects to some of the first type.

The most favoured type of canoeing lifejacket, approved by the B.C.U., fits over the head and has most of its bulk in front, with a strap around the waist. There is a solid block of buoyant material and additional buoyancy is obtained by mouth inflation. With no substantial part of the jacket at the sides, arm movements are not obstructed, and it is becoming customary for this type of lifejacket to be worn by canoeists, whether good swimmers or not, whenever they go afloat.

For normal use the uninflated jacket is not excessively bulky, yet it will support a conscious man and allow him to do things while in the water without having to go through the motions of swimming. It is possible to partly or completely inflate the jacket while in the water or in advance when bad conditions are expected.

Approval has not been given to aids which depend on air alone, so supports based on variations of the air cushion, which have been popular, are no longer officially advised although they may be quite efficient so long as they remain unpunctured. Similarly, kapok, which has been the standby of lifejacket manufacture for so long, is not approved unless it is in sealed plastic pockets. Most solid buoyancy is now provided by plastic foam.

An excess of personal buoyancy should be avoided. In some circumstances this could make it difficult for a canoeist to extricate himself from a capsized canoe.

Safety precautions which should always be observed are: the use of spray covers which will release without special effort; kit stowed so that the area around the legs is free; footwear which does not interfere with swimming; and a knowledge of the waters ahead, usually gained by inspection immediately beforehand.

When rapids of any size are tackled a throwing line may be valuable. It may be painter material although cotton and nylon are less likely to tangle. The length of rope depends on circumstances, but an average line, useful to a white-water party might be 50 ft. long and about 1 in. circumference.

Capsizing

The average type of touring canoe is extremely stable, and if the canoeist is tackling waters within his own capabilities the possibility of a capsize is extremely remote. As the canoe becomes more sporty, its inherent stability becomes less, but this is usually compensated for by the increased skill of the canoeist who chooses it. However, it is possible that a canoe will be capsized on the odd occasion—even if the probability is remote—and the competent canoeist is the one who knows what he will do if he capsizes and has practised it.

The ability to swim is essential for anyone who goes afloat in small craft. This is not peculiar to canoes, but is a common-sense requirement applicable to any small craft. The ability to swim long distances is not so important. All that is required is the ability to swim perhaps fifty yards, which gives confidence when in the water.

The rule next in importance is to leave the canoe inverted and stay with it until it can be got to shallow water. If an attempt is made to right it in deep water by its crew, the air lock inside will be broken and as the canoe turns the right way it will scoop up a considerable amount of water. Most of this will have to be baled out before the crew can climb

in. Climbing into a canoe from the water may make a good
interlude at a regatta, but it has no practical use in river
canoeing.

If a single-seater capsizes the canoeist should grab his
paddle and lay it along the keel if he can. If he cannot reach
it he should let it go. It is unwise to leave the canoe to swim
after it. He should go to one end of the canoe and swim with
it. If he favours a breast stroke, he should push the canoe. If
he prefers to swim on his back he should pull the canoe. If
it is a two-seater, each man should be at opposite ends.
Control of direction is probably better when pulling. When
pushing it is easier to see where you are going, but the action
of pushing one end raises the other and if there is any wind
it may catch it. If there is any current the ferry glide technique may be used to help get the canoe to the bank. Instead
of heading directly for the bank, the canoe should be pulled
by the swimmer so that it points diagonally upstream in the
direction he wishes to go. The current will then press against
the side of the canoe and assist his efforts.

If the capsize is in a rocky rapid it is best to let the inverted
canoe go first and to trail after it in as horizontal a position
as possible so as to avoid knocking the body on rocks. When
the worst is over the canoe can be directed into an eddy or
other shallow water.

When the inverted canoe has been got into water not more
than about knee deep it is best for two people to take the ends.
At first, most of the weight should be taken while turning the
canoe slightly so as to break the air lock inside by lifting one
side of the cockpit coaming above water level. Water will
then start running out. The canoe should be rocked from
side to side to assist the water out. If there is a considerable
amount of water inside, lifting should be only gradual when
the air lock has been broken, otherwise the pressure from
inside may burst the decks. Much of the weight should be
taken by the river, and lifting from the surface should be
regulated very gradually as the water pours out.

Resist strongly any offers of help from well-meaning but

ignorant onlookers who want to get the canoe on the bank. The canoe is probably undamaged because of the capsize, but if it is pulled out it may be ruined. Nearly all of the water should be emptied on the surface of the river, and only a gallon or less should be inside when the canoe is lifted on to the bank.

If a capsize has to be dealt with single-handed (although it is not good canoeing to get into this state without company) the canoe may be partially emptied in shallow water by grasping one end and jerking it upwards. The other end will be supported in a limited way by the water and some of the water inside will be released with each jerk.

If a second canoe is available to help at a capsize, the man in the water should get to one end, while the other canoeist takes him in tow. If he is able to use the painter of the capsized canoe he can bring it over the back of his cockpit and make it fast to a frame. Otherwise he will have to attach a line to the inverted canoe first. The point of a cockpit coaming in the water offers less resistance than the rear end, so it is usually better to tow bow first.

If a towing line cannot be attached, it is just possible to grasp the end of the canoe and paddle single-bladed with the other hand. In a two-seater the forward man can paddle while his partner holds the capsized canoe if he is unable to attach it by a line. If there is any flow, it is even more important for one canoe with another in tow to use a ferry glide to move crabwise across, facing upstream. Otherwise attempting to steer with a partially waterlogged canoe attached is well-nigh impossible.

If a canoe is used to rescue someone in the water, he should be instructed to hold on to the stern of the canoe but not to attempt to haul himself on to the stern deck, which may capsize the canoe.

At sea, or where the bank is too far away to consider swimming with the canoe to it, different methods must be used. The most important lifesaving equipment for a sea-going canoeist is at least one more canoe—in other words rescue after a capsize at sea is difficult unaided, and sea canoeing should only be done in a party. A lone canoeist who capsizes at sea in anything except calm conditions is unlikely to be able to bale his canoe and get on board again without help.

If a canoe has to be entered without help after a capsize, it will be necessary to right the canoe while swimming beside it. The keel or bilge keel may be pulled, so that the canoe is jerked upright quickly, before much water is scooped up. Most of the water must be baled before an attempt is made to enter the canoe. A plastic mug is useful for this. If there is much bilge water washing about, the canoe will be very unstable. The crew of a two-seater should be at opposite sides, and one member should steady the canoe while his mate pulls himself up and over the coaming into the cockpit. He then has the job of balancing the canoe while his companion does the same. It is not usually possible to get in from the side of a single-seater, as it is necessary to get the weight of the body across the cockpit in one jump. The only alternative is to straddle the stern deck and work up to the cockpit from the end. If the paddle is taken in front of you it becomes a sort of balancing pole, with the added advantage of sculling or other strokes to help.

A man being helped from another canoe should stay in the water until his canoe is ready, unless the other canoe is a large two-seater that can take him safely. He may use the other canoe for support, but he should not try to lift himself out of the water.

If there is one canoe assisting, the end of the capsized canoe may be lifted on to the deck of it. The man in the water can then go to the other end, set the canoe swinging from side to side and turn it over without scooping too much water into the cockpit. If there are two assisting canoes, it may be possible to get both ends of the capsized canoe on to the decks, so that the man in the water can pour out water by tilting gently and eventually righting the canoe. If the empty canoe is then held alongside an assisting canoe, more baling can be done and the canoe steadied while its crew enter.

Most Canadian canoes have so much beam and a stable cross-section that capsizing is unlikely, but because of their open form swamping, without actually turning over, is possible. Where the bank is near it is best to swim with the canoe to it without attempting to bale it. However, because of the absence of decking, a swamped Canadian canoe is easier to bale and enter in deep water. The canoe is rolled to the upright position, then one end is held and with a strong swimming stroke the canoe is thrust forward. Much of the water will come out over the swimmer, and he should raise the end as soon as the water ceases flowing. This may be done several times. Transfer to the side and rock by depressing the near gunwale, then kicking to raise it. Always the far gunwale is kept high. Water can be splashed over the near side. Boarding is possible on this stable craft by a leap across the gunwales providing the weight is dropped inside immediately.

Rule of the Road

A canoe is more vulnerable than almost anything else afloat, so in general a canoeist is best advised to keep out of the way of other craft. One rule which every canoeist should understand is that if two boats are meeting end on and there will be a collision if neither alters course, they both alter their course to starboard. This is not quite the same thing as saying that you keep to the right on a river. There is no need to keep to the right if you are not likely to collide with another boat—you merely go to the right if something else is coming directly towards you. Actually, on a river with any flow, it is easier to go upriver at the side and let downstream craft benefit by the faster centre stream.

All other craft give way to sail, so keep out of the way of yachts and dinghies. Large power craft have to keep to a rather narrow channel and cannot alter course, so give them the right of way. It is common courtesy for pleasure boats to avoid hindering the working boatman in any case.

Power craft use sound signals. The horn or hooter does not merely mean 'Look out, I am coming'. If you are canoeing in busy tidal waters, such as the Pool of London, the master of a tug is entitled to expect that you understand what he means when he gives a sound signal. He then makes the manœuvre indicated and cannot get out of your way, particularly if he is towing barges. The signals are:

1 blast: I am altering course to starboard (right).
2 blasts: 1 am altering course to port (left).
3 blasts: I am going astern.
4 blasts, followed by 1: I am turning about to starboard.
4 blasts, followed by 2: 1 am turning about to port.

A canoe at sea is almost invisible. To prevent collisions and to make it easier to find a canoeist in difficulties it is worth while considering colour schemes. The common silver or grey hull with a blue deck is the reverse of what is wanted. The colours most easily seen at sea are red and orange. If you use these for hull and deck you have done all you can to make your craft visible.

At night a canoeist is expected to carry a light which he can show when any other craft is approaching. Most night canoeists rely on an electric torch. It is unlikely that anyone on a large craft would see a canoe light in time to do anything, so at night the canoeist must keep a good look out all round.

The movements of other craft can be seen by their lights. Power craft have a red light to port and a green light to starboard, both showing forward and to their own side. There is also one or more white mast lights, and a white light showing astern. If you see both red and green lights the boat is coming towards you. If you only see one colour it is crossing and should not touch you. If you only see a white light it is going away from you. Yachts under sail only do not have the mast lights.

6

Sea Canoeing

MANY canoeists get their greatest enjoyment out of using their craft on the sea. There is an exhilaration about the moving water, different from rapid rivers and placid waters. The all-round canoeist practises all types of canoeing, but sea canoeing is not for the beginner. He should obtain experience on placid waters before tackling anything more advanced than a trip round a harbour or in a sheltered bay on a calm day; then he should make sure he is familiar with all the requirements of the ambitious sea canoeist.

If a beginner has an accident, discovers a flaw in his canoe, or merely feels too tired to go on, on inland placid waters, there is little to worry about and usually no immediate danger, but it is a different matter on the open sea. Serious sea canoeing is something to work up to, then, when the canoeist is confident in his craft and his own ability, it can be the cause of a great deal of satisfaction.

The requirements for satisfactory sea canoeing can be divided into four main groups:

1. A suitable canoe in good condition.
2. The strength and ability to paddle correctly for long periods.
3. A knowledge of basic seamanship.
4. Adequate safety precautions.

Most general-purpose touring canoes are suitable for sea work, and advice on their choice is given in Chapter 2. The canoe itself should be sound and its equipment should be beyond reproach. The constant buffeting of waves will find any weak points. Patches on the skin should be absolutely tight. Screwed fittings on folding canoes should be tightened with tools as well as by hand. The spray cover should do its job properly. You cannot get to the bank and make adjustments. You cannot even reach far under the deck to attend to kit stowage. Everything should be as near perfect as you can get it when you set off. A preliminary run in sheltered water is advisable.

It is most important that the sea canoeist should be in effect a paddling machine capable of keeping going for very long periods. A man or woman who is not in good physical condition should not take a canoe on tidal waters. General physical training will build up muscles, but the only really satisfactory training for canoeing is canoeing, so anyone contemplating extensive sea canoeing should get in all the paddling practice they can, on any sort of water.

The sea canoeist should be master of his canoe. He must be master of technique. He should be a capable paddler, able to use all the basic strokes, and able to appreciate what action to take in various circumstances, and do it instinctively. There may be no second chance to correct a wrongly performed stroke. Hence the need of plenty of practice on easy waters.

Seamanship is a vast subject, too great for much information to be given here, but several useful books are listed at the back of this book. Most important is the realization that the sea is always moving, both up and down in waves and swell, and horizontally in tidal streams. As the water may be moving much faster than a canoeist can paddle, an understanding of tides is essential. Using a tide can add considerably to distance covered and ease of paddling. Trying to go against the tide may result in no progress or worse.

Around the British Isles there is high water at rather more than twelve-hour intervals, with low water usually about seven hours after high water. When the moon is full or new there are spring tides, when the water rises exceptionally high and drops exceptionally low. Midway between come neap tides, with a lesser range. The main tidal stream from the Atlantic is divided around the British Isles, part going up the West coast and part up the Channel. Tide-tables are published, usually giving times at certain ports and constants to be added or subtracted to get the times at other ports. The set of tidal streams are given on charts. Admiralty charts are published for larger craft, but there are special yachtsman's charts, which are useful to canoeists.

Tidal streams are not always simple. In the same way as the water in a rapid river eddies around rocks and swirls back into hollows in the bank, the streams are affected by the coast and the sea-bed. The Isle of Wight divides a stream and causes double high water in the Solent area. Headlands can be particularly dangerous to small craft, as streams may meet at some states of the tide, causing overfalls. The race off Portland Bill is a well-known example. Where the tide is forced through a narrow channel it may become very fast. When flowing over a shallow bar, as there is at the entrance to many harbours, the confused seas may be a considerable hazard to a canoe.

Waves at sea are always moving. In a rapid, the water moves, but the wave is stationary. In deep water, there is a regular swell, which may have quite high crests, but these are at long intervals and no great danger to a canoe. It is the shorter and sharper seas which are of more concern to the canoeist. So long as a wave is not breaking it can be negotiated by the skilled sea canoeist. but once the top starts curling over, due to the strength of the wind or the shallow bottom, it is difficult to prevent being turned off your course or capsized.

The sea canoeist should automatically observe the safety precautions described in Chapter 5. His buoyancy bags and lifejacket should be in first-class condition and checked immediately before setting out. His painters will be secure

—short of going over the side after it, he cannot do anything if one starts trailing. A spare paddle is almost essential. This may be in halves on the deck, with the blades in pockets forward and the looms held by straps each side of the coaming. If there is any choice, it is worth while having a stouter and heavier paddle, as the strain at sea is much more than elsewhere.

An unloaded canoe may be almost too buoyant and not sufficiently immersed in the water. Normally there will be some kit stowed, and this weight distributed throughout the canoe makes it steadier and easier to keep on a course. All kit should be fixed in place, and care must be taken to avoid making the canoe heavier by the bow than the stern, as this makes steering very difficult. Anything likely to be needed during the trip should be stowed within reach, usually at the sides of the seat. Even if the trip is only expected to be for an hour or so, food and drink should be carried. Chocolate and glucose sweets, and a fruit drink are appreciated. Maybe their immediate effect physically is negligible, but they boost morale during a hard spell.

Navigation is largely a matter of advance preparation— there cannot be much chart work during the trip. A small compass on a bracket over a side deck will give a clue to direction. Bearings can be found before starting. The compass helps you to keep on course if conditions become misty. A folded chart, or a list of bearings, distances, prominent landmarks and similar information, may be in a transparent plastic container within view, possibly fastened to the spray cover. Buoys which can be identified should be known.

Local advice will be useful, but make sure that the man asked knows what he is talking about—not every man in a blue jersey is an expert. Advance knowledge of possible landing places is most important. You should know where to make for if you have to get ashore at any stage of the trip. This is not always simple. It is possible for conditions to be fit for reasonably safe canoeing away from the shore long after landing on an open beach has become impossible. If a beach shelves steeply there will be an undertow which may drown even a good swimmer.

Usually the wind is not blowing straight on shore and in a bay one end may be more sheltered than the other. Landing and embarking may be simpler there. Getting afloat off an open beach can be wet, even in calm conditions. The canoe may be straddled and dropped into as a wave lifts it, or it may be pushed to deeper water and entered in the normal way from wading. The complication is the need for action almost immediately, so the paddle must be ready, and strokes made even before you are settled comfortably. When landing the greatest difficulty may be in keeping the canoe straight. Swinging sideways may mean overturning. Progress will usually be slower than the waves. This will mean a certain amount of solid water coming over the stern. This will have to be accepted as backwatering into a wave is the best way of keeping straight. Some two-seaters come ashore better if paddled stern first! In rough conditions a wetting must be accepted, and the best way may be to go over the side near shore and wade with the painter held in the hand.

Whenever possible the canoe should be entered and left in a sheltered place, preferably from a bank, steps, ramp or similar place. Rocks may have possibilities, but with the constant movement of the water, the risk of damaging the canoe should be watched. Help may be useful, providing the helpers understand what they are to do. Paddling children may be a menace, even if they are trying to be helpful.

In open water a long steady stroke should be adopted, as far as possible. Keeping a course diagonal to wind and sea is the most difficult. The inexperienced paddler will do a lot of back paddling. Some may be necessary, but it represents negative effort and should be kept to a minimum. It will be necessary to turn the bow up into the larger waves, and progress on the course resumed as soon as the wave has passed, then as much distance made good as possible before the next delaying large wave. A foot-operated rudder reduces the amount of negative paddling which will have to be done, so that the best use can be made of the power expended.

In general it is better to keep in reasonably deep water than to creep along close inshore when on a passage. In particular a rocky coast should be avoided. Apart from rocks close to the surface, the water thrown back is confused. Farther offshore the movement of the water is more regular.

When you are canoeing inland it is unlikely that anyone will be concerned with you officially. When you tackle coastal canoeing you will come under observation by the coastguards. Any craft afloat is their concern. They are particularly concerned about your safety. This is very gratifying, but it can be embarassing. There have been occasions when a lifeboat has been called out to a canoeist who has actually not been in any danger. For your own safety and the peace of mind of others, you should tell the coastguards where you are going and when if you plan a coastal passage. Remember to tell them if you alter your plans, and tell them when you have completed the trip. If you are working from a base and making trips daily, a general indication of what is happening will ensure the helpful co-operation of the coastguards. You should also tell others at your base, and give them more details, particularly your estimated time of return.

Sea canoeing has to be learned by practice, rather than from a book. Tackled in the right spirit and with expeditions kept within your known limitations, it is a very satisfying and enjoyable branch of the sport. The upper waters of an estuary can give the feel of tidal waters, then trips may be made at the mouth of a river, or in a landlocked harbour, while nautical knowledge is acquired, before passages are made in open water in the right conditions. In capable hands a decked canoe is a surprisingly seaworthy craft, as proved by large numbers of Channel crossings and two Atlantic crossings.

7

Competitive Canoeing

THERE are several types of competition in canoes:

1. Straightforward racing over standard distances in calm water.
2. Long-distance racing, involving hazards and varying conditions.
3. Rag events, in which racing is not treated as seriously and the canoes are of the ordinary touring type.
4. Slalom, in which the competitors negotiate an obstacle course in white water.
5. Kandahar or rapid-river racing, in which a slalom may be included.
6. Sailing, in specialist canoes, as described in Chapter 10.

Racing

First-class racing is in special canoes conforming to the specifications laid down by the International Canoe Federation. Racing canoes propelled by double-bladed paddles are described as kayaks, which is abbreviated to 'K' with a number indicating the number of crew:

K1 Maximum length: 520 cm. (17 ft. 0·72 in.)
Minimum breadth: 51 cm. (20·08 in.)
Minimum weight: 12 kilos. (26·46 lb.)

K2 Maximum length: 650 cm. (21 ft. 3·90 in.)
Minimum breadth: 55 cm. (21·65 in.)
Minimum weight: 18 kilos. (39·68 lb.)

K4 Maximum length: 1100 cm. (36 ft. 1·07 in.)
    Minimum breadth: 60 cm. (23·62 in.)
    Minimum weight: 30 kilos. (66·14 lb.)

All methods of construction are permitted, but the majority of these craft are built of wood veneers, giving a light and smooth skin. Glassfibre is used, but is much heavier. The beam is at the gunwales, and it is possible to make this much narrower on the waterline by having concave lines above (Fig. 15G), but there is a rule that all lines should be convex.

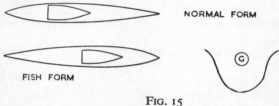

NORMAL FORM

FISH FORM

FIG. 15
Racing-canoe forms

While the basic technique is the same as for using a touring canoe, the racing paddler has a canoe which is very responsive and needs balancing. As it is narrower and lower, the paddle is shorter and with larger blades. Strokes are made close to the side of the canoe, consequently the blade in the air is lifted much higher.

The paddler needs a firm moulded seat and a strong rest for his feet, as the thrust can be considerable. The cockpit coaming is shaped so that the knees may be braced against it. A rudder is used, usually a short distance in from the stern and only about the size of a playing card. Various methods of control have been used. A rigid heelrest and a pivoted rudder bar may be moved by the ball of the feet. A more popular arrangement has a footrest taking the soles of the feet and a tiller projecting over the rest, so that it can be pushed sideways by the feet. A light spray cover may be used, mainly to prevent wind slowing down the canoe by blowing into the cockpit, but most racing canoeists do not have one. In a two-seater or a four-seater it is usual for the front paddler to steer. Each paddler has a separate cockpit.

Racing Canadian canoes used for international competition are open for most of their length and without the characteristic upswept ends of the touring canoe. The limiting sizes are:

C1   Maximum length: 520 cm. (17 ft. 0·72 in.)
      Minimum breadth: 75 cm. (29·5 in.)
      Minimum weight: 20 kilos.

C2   Maximum length: 650 cm. (21 ft. 3·90 in.)
      Minimum breadth: 75 cm. (29·5 in.)
      Minimum weight: 20 kilos.

In both cases decking may extend 150 cm. from the bow and 75 cm. at the stern. Rudders are not allowed.

The paddle used for racing a Canadian canoe is long and spadelike. The paddler(s) kneel near the centre of the canoe on the knee the same side as the paddle is used. The canoe tilts slightly away from the paddling side and the stroke is very long. Not much first-class racing is done in Britain in Canadian canoes.

Although first-class racing normally takes place in light wooden K1, K2 and K4 craft, these are now very expensive canoes, and much training and local racing is in glass-fibre canoes, which are the same shape externally and more robust. They are not quite as fast, but they are considerably cheaper. For junior racing there have been several designs approved and recognised by the British Canoe Union to suit young people. For some time there were single and two-seat kayaks built of plywood and designated 'National Chine Kayaks', but these have fallen from favour and most junior racing is in glass-fibre slightly scaled-down versions of the normal K craft, or young people race in the full-size kayaks.

In recent years there have been many experiments in the

shapes and sizes of kayaks and races are often organised
to suit particular designs. Obviously if the craft are identical,
sport can be just as good, even if the kayaks do not conform
to any special standard.

Races are usually over 500, 1000 and 10,000 metres.
Women's events are 500 metres only. Canoe events are
included in the Olympic Games (every four years). World
Championships are held midway between the Olympic
Games, and European Championships in the intervening
years. National Championships are held every year, and
most clubs hold regattas, which may include open events.

Long-distance racing
A number of long-distance races are recognized as ranking
events by the British Canoe Union, the club gaining the
highest number of points each year holds the Hasler
Trophy. The recognized races vary from inland placid
rivers, such as the Leamington River Race, which is twelve
miles with four portages; to the Poole Harbour Race, which
is thirteen miles, mostly in open tidal waters. These races
are organized by local clubs on behalf of the British Canoe
Union. All kinds of canoes take part in these events and
there are many classes to cater for most types.

Races are arranged to suit Seniors, Juniors and Ladies
in almost any type of canoe. In most races Juniors and
Ladies race over shortened courses. The classes which attract
the experts are those restricted to first-class canoes of
the same types as used for straightforward racing. K and
other canoes race in their own classes. Other classes cover
the main types of touring canoes, both single and two
seaters.

Of course, the specialist racing craft are not the best for
races involving portages and rough conditions. There has
been much experiment to find the best canoes for this com-

paratively new type of racing, resulting in the development of craft between the extreme racers and the accepted touring types. One possible result is the realization that a canoe narrower than has been usual may be satisfactory in bad conditions, when its crew are sufficiently skilful. This is reflected in the use of slimmer canoes for touring, giving the experienced paddler more sport and speed, while still being sufficiently stable for his safety and comfort.

Long-distance racing has a wider appeal than ordinary racing. The technique is more that of the good touring canoeist.

The best-known long-distance race is not a ranking one —the annual Devizes–Westminster race at Easter, along the Kennet and Avon Canal, then down the Thames to London. This is a gruelling test of endurance, involving a large number of portages as well as canoeing ability, and watermanship to arrange the arrival at Teddington so as to take advantage of the tide.

Rag events

Short-distance events for touring canoes are usually staged at club regattas, together with club championships over greater distances. The programme usually includes several events in which the accent is on the entertainment of the audience. To keep the events within view it is common to start and finish at the same point, letting most races be around a buoy. This also reduces the number of officials, as the starters may also judge. Other essential officials are marshals to get competitors ready, a secretary to keep records, stewards afloat to act as referees and safety men, and an officer-of-the-day, who settles disputes. To be a success the regatta must be kept moving, and long gaps between races avoided. Alternating single and double events helps.

Slalom

This form of rough-water contest, with a name borrowed from skiing, is mainly a post-war development, although a few slaloms had been held pre-war. The course consists of obstacles, made by hanging poles from ropes. Colours and signs indicate how the 'gates' are to be negotiated. The course is laid out over broken water, and the canoeist's skill is shown in the way he is able to weave through the course, attempting to pass through all the gates without touching them.

The canoes are specialist craft—single-seater kayaks, shorter than most tourers and designed to manœuvre quickly. Cockpits are small, and the canoe is easily rolled. For first-class slaloms the international rules say that the kayaks should fold. In Britain there are divisions, based on points gained in ranking slaloms, and for divisions other than the first, rigid canoes may be used. Canadian canoes are also used in slalom, although their development for this purpose is mainly continental.

A slalom course is laid out on a natural rapid river, or on one where a weir or sluice gives rapid water conditions. A weir slalom tends to be small in extent, with the route compressed by crossing. A river slalom may be much more extensive. Because of the compact form of a slalom it has become more of a spectacle, and this type of canoeing has become better known to the layman, particularly through the medium of television.

In a slalom there is only one competitor on the course at a time, except in team events. His progress is timed, and there are judges at each gate to give him penalty times if he touches or misses. The run is void if the canoeist capsizes and leaves his canoe, so most slalom enthusiasts learn to roll. With each competitor allowed two runs, a large slalom can occupy many officials for a considerable time.

Possibly in slalom more than any other form of canoeing it is important for the canoeist and his craft to act as one. The seat is low and comes around the body, there are knee-grips and the feet press down firmly. The spray cover is close-fitting, and the canoe responds to every movement.

Interest in slalom has increased considerably in recent years, so much so that it was introduced into the Olympic Games in 1972. In Britain and other countries slaloms are arranged to suit different grades of ability. Technique is now of a very high order and the ways of the experts in dealing with white water are being learned by more general canoeists, so that canoeing standards throughout the sport and pastime are far better today.

Rapid-river racing

Maybe if slalom had not attracted the white-water enthusiasts, there would have been more interest in rapid-river racing, but this is not popular in Britain. Competitors may be started at intervals and timed. What preliminary and advance inspection may be permitted must be decided by the organizers. Adequate safety precautions must be taken, and competitors may wear crash-helmets as well as life-jackets. The events are more popular on the Continent, where suitable rivers are larger. The Arkansas River Race in the U.S.A. attracts an international entry, and the annual Maritzburg–Durban race in South Africa adds snakes to the other hazards.

A British event not strictly a race, but akin to it, is the Leven White-Water Test, organized by the Lakeland Canoe Club and arranged at intervals. There are many rapids in a short length of the Leven as it runs out of Lake Windermere. Bogey times have been worked out and canoeists compete against them for badges indicating their degree of success. The badge is in the form of a dipper, which is a small local bird able to swim under water.

8

White Water

THE canoe is a more suitable craft for tackling rapid rivers than any other form of boat. To many the rapid river, with a variety of hazards, is the main reason for their attraction to canoeing. Certainly, more skill may be developed and used than in any other branch of canoeing. The beginner may also enjoy playing white water, providing he starts with easy grades and progresses to the rougher waters as he becomes experienced, and preferably under the leadership of someone more skilled.

All rivers finding their way to the sea have ploughed out their own bed. When the fall is only slight in a stretch of water, it usually flows sluggishly and deep, but when the fall is greater, the speed is more and the bed will be worn away unevenly; the soft spots becoming holes, while the hard rocks project, often through the surface. The water then froths and bubbles, there are waves with broken tops, and we have what is collectively termed 'white water'.

Britain is too small to have very large rapid rivers, but those that flow out of the hills can offer sport for short distances, and the usual white-water river consists of long comparatively placid stretches between shorter lengths of exciting water. In larger countries there may be stretches of white water needing several days to traverse. In these large rivers the volume of water may be the greatest hazard. In a smaller river it is the rocks and other obstructions which are the main danger.

There is an international system of river grading which

13. The hectic start of a long-distance race for young people

14. A typical easy rapid where the water is broken by falling over a shingle bar—on the Severn near Bewdley

15. A telemark turn

(A) The canoeist leans on to the paddle which is making a sculling stroke and turns the canoe on edge

(B) From the other side the rockered effect presented to the water can be seen as the canoe tilts

16. International K2 kayaks being used in a long-distance race on the River Exe in Devon

17. Demonstrating how the sculling action may be used to prevent a capsize. Note knees gripped under deck

18. A slalom canoeist pulls his canoe around with a high telemark; a more sophisticated version of the stroke shown in plate 12

gives a clue to the degree of difficulty. This can only be a guide, as there are so many variables. Differences in water level can make a considerable difference in the characteristics of the river. As it is impossible to have one standard for comparison gradings are not always uniform, as they have been allocated according to different observer's personal opinions. However, the grading should always be noted when assessing the practicability of a particular river. Of course, many rivers have stretches of various grades.

The white-water grades are:

I *Easy*. Small regularly spaced waves. Minor hazards. Channels easily found.

II *Medium*. Fairly easy frequent rapids, with regular waves, and small eddies or whirlpools. Channels fairly easy to find.

III *Difficult*. Numerous rapids, often with irregular waves, breakers and confused water. Best passage not always easy to find.

IV *Very Difficult*. Lengthy rapids, with large waves, much broken water and difficult hazards. Best passage difficult to find.

V *Exceedingly difficult*. Long unbroken stretches of rapids with difficult and irregular broken water, rocks, difficult whirlpools and fast eddies. Must be surveyed from the shore.

VI *Absolute limit of difficulty*. All difficulties increased to the limit of practicability, and cannot be attempted without great risk of life.

Beginners who have mastered their canoes and can control them on placid waters should be able to tackle grades I and II rivers, providing they are in company and are prepared to spend some time examining hazards before attempting them. Progress to grade III rivers is best done

under an experienced leader, but anyone who has gained
confidence on rivers of lower grades and is prepared to
observe all reasonable safety precautions should find they
are capable of dealing with them. The higher grades are
more hazardous and should only be tackled with an understanding of what is involved. However, rougher stretches
are usually restricted to comparatively short distances and
it is often possible to portage or line down.

Reading white water

A rapid occurs where the bed of the river slopes more
steeply or where there are constrictions in its width. Frequently both conditions are present—there is a definitely
increased angle to the bed and either the banks close in or
there are islands or other obstructions reducing the effective
width of the river (Plate 11). Unfortunately there is only
the one word for describing everything from the slight
speeding on a mainly placid river to the impossible raging
torrent. The Canadians use the word 'riffle' for the little
ones, and this name deserves wider use.

In flowing at a greater speed the water produces various
effects which the skilled canoeist can learn to interpret.
Much of this knowledge can only come by experience, but
a useful start can be made by looking at the problem
theoretically. The same effects can be seen in little streams
as in large rivers, and much can be learned by watching
the water in a fast brook. Variations in the bed have the
same effect and the behaviour of the water can be seen.
Early practice of white-water techniques can be in rivers
which the expert would hardly call rapid, but water behaviour can be studied more leisurely and the worst result
of a miscalculation is likely to be a wade ashore.

Fortunately nature has provided one effect in almost
every rapid which the beginner can soon learn to interpret.
In making its way down the rapid the water finds the
deepest or easiest channel and proceeds to flow fastest
through it, ploughing it deeper and washing away loose

stones. This main channel is marked by a V of smooth water at the top, with the point of the V directing you into the centre of the channel. There may be more than one channel, but almost certainly one V will be much bigger than the rest. In most cases this is the best way down, but you must first check on obstructions either in the water or trees with branches hanging close to the water. It is not always easy to see where the V is when you are approaching in a canoe, and landing to inspect is advisable.

Other effects caused by rocks under the surface are not so easy for the beginner to read. At first it is a safe rule to avoid any breaking water. If the top of a wave is curling over there is something not far below the surface. It may be far enough down to miss the canoe, but at first the canoeist should regard every breaking top as danger.

Waves in a rapid differ from those at sea by being station-ary. At sea the whole body of water is moving and the waves are travelling in a pattern. In a rapid the water is flowing and waves are caused by this flow hitting an obstruction. The effect of the obstruction is modified by a number of factors, such as the depth and speed, and the volume of water flowing. In a simple case the water hits the obstruc-tion and is forced upwards. If there is considerable depth or little flow the effect is ironed out between the rock and the surface (Fig. 16A) and the obstruction is no hazard and not even noticed by a canoeist. If the water is shallower the bump caused by the water being forced upwards appears as a wave on the surface (Fig. 16B). The wave may swing slightly with variations in the flow, but it is always over the same area. If the rock is very close to the surface or actually breaking through it, the water will not continue its smooth flow, but will be broken up into drops and spray (Fig. 16C).

With the same size rock and the same depth, the speed of the water can cause different effects. The rock which causes only a smooth bump at 3 m.p.h. may cause a broken wave at 10 m.p.h. Variations in water level can alter the characteristics of a rapid considerably. It is never advisable

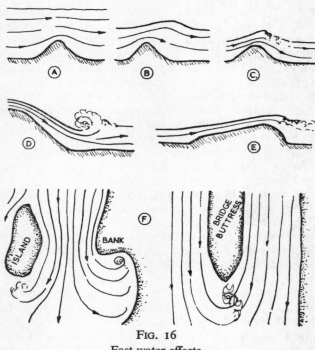

FIG. 16
Fast-water effects

to assume that because you have been down a rapid before
it will be the same. In all but the simplest, inspection is
advisable every time. Of course, deeper water usually means
an easier passage, but if you are looking for sport, inspection
may show you subsidiary channels which would be more
fun than the main one, yet were impassable or not even there
in lower water. Lower water will almost certainly bring
rocks near the surface causing new waves and possibly
altering the flow of the main stream.

Not all waves are caused by rocks. Waterlogged tree
branches are a common hazard in British rivers. Fortunately

they usually settle pointing downstream, so that if you hit one you have a good chance of bouncing off undamaged. If there is much flow and the branch is entirely submerged, the wave caused is likely to be narrower and possibly diagonal to the general flow, deflecting the current slightly. In this case the top of the wave may be broken slightly, due to the deflected water being hit over by the water flowing straight. A branch just breaking the surface can catch the unwary. The water may be otherwise deep enough and if the flow is rather slight the telltale wave as the water builds up behind the branch and is deflected around it may not be obvious. The piled-up water hides the actual branch as you approach it.

Even more dangerous is the old bedstead or spiked gate, which takes up a similar position. If you are canoeing where civilization (!) uses the river as a dump for its rubbish, this sort of thing is by no means a negligible hazard.

A large wave may be caused merely by fast water hitting a patch of deep still water. The effect then is for the fast water to curl back on itself (Fig. 16D). When the canoe hits one of these small 'stoppers' or 'haystacks' it ploughs through. If it hits a larger one you paddle hard to get through. If you hit a really big one, it stops you and throws you back.

Flat rocks can be a nuisance. Their frequency depends on the formation of the river-bed, but usually they are not apparent until your canoe comes to rest on them. The shallow water over them piles up slightly and any telltale broken water downstream is hidden until you are past (Fig. 16E).

Eddies and whirlpools are caused by the water changing speed and turning back behind the shelter of a rock, bridge buttress or bay in the bank (Fig. 16F). On the average British river these are not large enough to be dangerous, unless you are caught unawares and the canoe spins round unexpectedly.

Another water effect, particularly towards the end of summer, is that caused by weeds. Of course, weeds below the surface are no hazard, but they can cause waves which may be mistaken for those caused by rocks. Masses of weeds growing at a considerable length from the bottom will be bent by the flow of water and take up a position hanging downstream and swinging in the current. A thick group which has nearly reached the surface can cause quite a large wave. However, where the flow is great enough to cause a wave the weeds will usually be swinging from side to side. This causes the wave to also swing from side to side. As no rock would be moving about, the observant canoeist interprets a swinging wave correctly as being caused by weeds, and therefore safe to pass over.

In low-water conditions towards the end of a dry summer weeds can almost block what would otherwise be shallow simple rapids. There may still be a V showing the best way into the mass, but the passage after that may be far from straight. The weeds will show you where to go as they will be bent in the direction of the flow. By following the bent weeds it may be possible to find a tortuous route through, when otherwise you would be wading.

Weirs

A weir, as a hazard to canoeists, often needs more care and inspection than the beginner may realize. A seemingly simple fall may be a more dangerous obstacle than is at first realized. The safest rule for a beginner, or even anyone moderately experienced, is to portage or line down every weir.

A weir differs from a rapid in being a sudden drop. It may be natural, with the water falling over a confusion of boulders and rocks, or man-made, with a comparatively straight sill and either a vertical drop or a more gradual slope down to the lower level. The drop may be only a few inches, or it may be many feet. As its details cannot be seen from the upriver approach, a weir should always be inspected from the bank. This means landing well in advance. If there is much water going over the weir, the surface of the river will speed up before and if you approach too close before attempting to land you may be swept over. A weir ahead may usually be identified first by the deepening water, then by its noise, and the river will appear to come to a stop with a line across the river.

If shooting is contemplated, check that there is ample water over the top of the weir. If your stern lodges on the sill you are not likely to stay upright. If it is a man-made weir, look for iron rods and similar obstructions. The makers of weirs did not expect boats to pass over them and the surface is not necessarily smooth. This can be a hazard even when lining down.

A fairly abrupt drop of a few feet, with plenty of water going over, may offer sport, but it is hazardous. A more gradual slope will be less trouble. When a part of the canoe is out of its element, particularly when you are supported by the ends, balance is difficult.

The greatest dangers are below the weir. Many things are washed over the weir. Waterlogged trees tend to lodge at the bottom, where they cannot be seen below the waves. Examine the wave formation at the bottom of the weir. The main body of water plunges deep, while more water above it curls back continuously towards the weir. If a stick is thrown in it will be seen to float towards the weir and disappear under the water, to reappear at the downriver end of the wave and start floating back again. If this stopper wave is small, a canoe may thrust through it, but if it is bigger the effect of hitting it will be an abrupt stop and a probable swing broadside before a capsize. The canoeist will then be rolled towards the weir and under the surface. The only way out is to continue under water and hope to be carried far enough downriver to be clear of the stopper wave when you reach the surface.

A natural weir will probably have breaks through which the water flows like a rapid. Some man-made weirs have breaks with a similar water flow. Some were actually built in that way to help salmon going upriver. The flow here will be greater than elsewhere and the slope will be much more reasonable. There will be a V of smooth water pointing the way, but someone to shout direction is advisable; then this may be a reasonably safe and exciting way down.

However—if you have the slightest doubt at a weir, portage or line down.

White-water technique

When white water is met, there will probably be several hazards in a group, and the proposed route through must be planned when examining from the shore. Normally, if there is a curve, the deeper water will be on the outside of the bend. Shallows may extend farther than is immediately obvious on the inside of the bend. If the river floods in the winter the bank on the outside of the bend may be undercut and a real danger if the canoe hits it. Tree branches dragging in the water can cause more difficulty than may be expected.

Mastery of the basic paddling strokes is essential in white-water canoeing. There are many combinations of them. Slalomists have given these special names, usually after successful exponents of them. The most important requirement is the ability to read the water, notice what it is doing and how parts of the canoe may be in water of different speeds; then to act so that the combination of stroke and water pressure gets the desired result.

It is wrong to merely drift with the current in white water. If the canoe is not moving in relation to the water, even if it is travelling quite fast past the bank, there will be no steerage way, and several strokes may be needed to get the canoe moving to change direction, and by then the movement may be too late. If there is a good depth, a straightforward rapid should be entered paddling forward. If it is shallow backwatering may be used, so that the canoe is not travelling as fast as the water. In that case any change of direction will be made stern first. In shoals, if the bottom is touched while backwatering, the hit will be gentle, and you step out, grasping the stern painter as you do so, ready to wade after your lightened canoe. If the canoe slews as it grounds, step out on the upriver side, otherwise as it lifts it may float against your legs and push you over.

A manœuvre that should be mastered is the ferry glide. This is a method of crossing fast water, using the water pressure to do the work. It is named after current-operated ferries which are tethered by a cable and set at an angle to the current by their rudder so that the water pressure against the side pushes them crabwise across the river. Once mastered, ferry glides may be used frequently in negotiating confused white water. It is possible to get near the sill of a weir to inspect it, then move sideways to the part where you will shoot it; or when the main current on a curve sets under an overhanging bank to pull away from it and out of danger. It is particularly valuable when the current is setting through tree branches. Trying to turn and paddle in the normal way may result in the canoe being swept broadside into them, with a capsize and considerable danger to the canoeist.

To perform a ferry glide, stop the canoe by backwatering until you are stationary in relation to the current (Fig. 17A). Turn the stern in the direction you wish to go (Fig. 17B), then hold it at this angle to the current by back-paddling (Fig. 17C). The current will press against the side of the canoe and glance off, pushing the canoe across the river (Fig. 17D). As the current may vary, it may be necessary to alter the angle as you cross—a more acute angle (Fig. 17E) will be needed in the fast centre of the current than at the sides. (Fig. 17F). When you reach the position you want, you straighten up (Fig. 17G) and go forward. This may be practised anywhere that the water flows at more than about 3 m.p.h., and the effect is better seen if you try it facing upstream, although that direction is rarely needed in a rapid.

Another useful accomplishment is the telemark turn. Simple turning is done by paddling harder on one side, or

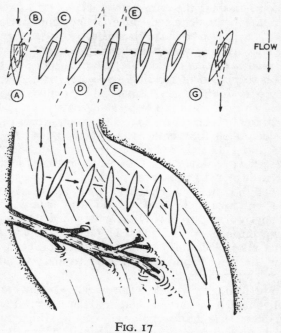

FIG. 17
A ferry glide

by alternately paddling backwards on the other side. With the usual straight-keeled canoe, turning is much quicker if the canoe is heeled, either way. As the lowest point of the canoe is now somewhere around the turn of the bilge, the effective keel has become very rockered, or swept up at the ends, making the canoe much more manœuvrable. In the telemark turn the canoe is heeled over and at the same time braked with the paddle held well out on the inside of the turn. Some canoes telemark better than others, but in any case the canoe must be moving fast. The paddle blade has to support the canoeist as well as brake the canoe, so it must be at an angle rather like a sculling stroke. An expert will telemark until the gunwale is under, then pull himself upright by pressing the blade forward in a sculling stroke (Plate 12).

A high telemark is a variation which cannot be used as often, but which is even more effective. The canoeist leans back as far as possible, with the paddle above his head, then leans and makes the braking stroke. With the centre of gravity lower and the stroke nearer the stern a greater turn is made for the same effort, and it is easier to follow with a forward stroke.

9

Canoe Building and Maintenance

THE majority of canoeists today build their own craft. Apart from the economy involved, there is a tremendous satisfaction in going afloat in a boat you have built yourself.

Many home builders tackle lath and canvas construction, which is simplest and does not require many tools or equipment (Fig. 18A). Frames are made from marine plywood. These and the end posts are mounted on a central lengthwise hog, with waterproof glue and screws. This assembly is temporarily clamped to a stiff plank, then the other lengthwise parts fitted. The framework is varnished, then covered with fabric. The hull material is pulled over the gunwales and tacked inside, then the deck tacked outside and covered with a rubbing strip. Cockpit coaming, bottom boards, seats and backrests complete the job. Altogether the complete job totals about four working days for two men or women. Most of the canoes pictured in this book are built in this way.

A folding canoe looks very similar when assembled (Fig. 18B), but materials for it cost much more, and greater skill is needed in building it. The lengthwise parts have joints so that it will pack, usually into a quarter of the full length. This involves some metalworking. The skin is a stout rubberized material, which has to be sewn to the deck canvas. Some folding canoe manufacturers will make skins to fit amateur-built folding frameworks.

Wood may have less skin friction than fabric, and can be faster, but plywood is the usual wood skin material

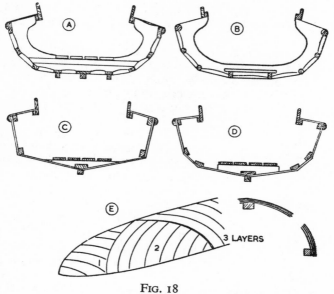

FIG. 18
Constructional methods

today, and as this cannot be bent in two directions at once, the advantage of smoothness may be cancelled out by the limitations of shape. Traditionally, wooden boats were built with clinker or carvel planking (Fig. 3), but canoes are rarely built this way today. Canoes built from plywood have the curve in the length and are hard-chine (Fig. 18C). They could be nearer a rounded section if made double-chine (Fig. 18D). Building in plywood calls for more wood-working skill and may take twice as long as lath and canvas.

Canoes of a good shape may be made by the moulded plywood method, in which the hull is built up of layers of veneer arranged in strips over a mould (Fig. 18E). Three layers held together with a waterproof glue provide sufficient strength for internal structural members to be unnecessary.

The mould must be accurately made, and the process is more suitable for quantity-production, when the preliminary work is justified.

Glass-reinforced plastic has much to commend it as a tough, durable and smooth material for boat building. An accurate mould has to be made, then the work is messy and costly for a one-off job. Although not impossible at home, the process is much more suited to quantity-production.

Plywood and glassfibre have been combined in canoe construction. The joints of a hard-chine plywood hull are covered with glass mat bedded in synthetic resin. Glassfibre bottoms have been moulded on to plywood sides.

Materials

Traditional boatbuilding is a skilled trade, but development of new materials has brought new methods which need much less skill. The biggest help in modern boatbuilding is synthetic resin glue. There are many types used in industry and a few available in small quantities for amateurs. The resin is set by a hardener and is then very strong and fully waterproof.

The resins used in glassfibre work are akin to the glues. The glass is in the form of a mat or cloth. It is best to buy all the materials needed from one specialist firm.

Ordinary animal glue should not be used on a boat. Marine glue is not an adhesive, but is the name given to a seam filler. Casein glue is a water-resistant glue now outclassed for boatbuilding by synthetic resins.

Plywood for boatbuilding is bonded with synthetic resin glue. In Britain standard sheets are 8 ft. × 4 ft. and marked 'B.S.S. 1088', indicating the boatbuilding grade. Thickness may be metric, when 9 mm. may be assumed to be ⅜ in.— the usual canoe frame thickness. A possible alternative is marked 'Exterior'.

Solid wood used in canoes should be light in weight. The favourite for lengthwise parts is Sitka spruce. Cheaper softwoods may be used, such as deal or parana pine, providing they are straight-grained and free from large knots. Some light hardwoods, such as ramin and maranti, are suitable. Varnished mahogany looks good and is favoured for coamings. For parts which have to be bent, ash is the only satisfactory easily obtained wood. It is used for bent frames in a rigid canoe and for most of the parts of a folding canoe.

The fastenings in a canoe should resist corrosion. The best screws are made of gunmetal, but ordinary brass screws are cheaper and satisfactory. Brass nails are also used. Copper boat nails have many uses (Fig. 19). The nail is driven through and a conical washer, called a 'rove', driven over the end, which is cut off and riveted.

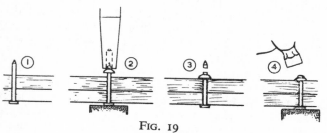

FIG. 19
Boat nails and roves

Skins of rigid canoes have usually been canvas, proofed and of about 15 oz. grade, painted after fixing. The deck canvas may be a lighter grade. The newer alternatives to ordinary canvas are plastics on a fabric base. These have good resistance to abrasion and are smoother and faster than canvas. Unbacked plastic is not advised. The material chosen must have a slight stretch in the length. Folding-canoe skins are usually five-ply (3 rubber, 2 canvas). This is expensive, but the only material to stand up to frequent folding.

Paint used on a canoe may be a marine grade or a good

household quality. Varnish should be a marine grade, preferably of a synthetic type.

Actual building costs depend on available materials and may be reduced if several craft are tackled at the same time. Kits, in which some of the work is done for you, naturally cost more, but they save time and may help the hesitant beginner. If the cost of the cheapest rigid canoe (11 ft. fabric-covered single-seater) is taken as £7, a 14 ft. single-seater will cost about £9 and a 15 ft. two-seater about £12. Plywood for one canoe would cost about £2 more, but for a quantity there would not be much difference. For glassfibre the mould would cost about the same as a fabric-covered canoe, then each canoe off it would cost about twice as much. Folding-canoe materials cost between two and three times as much as for fabric-covered rigid canoes.

There is no room in this book for detailed instructions on building canoes, but the author will be glad to supply information on plans available to any reader who writes to him (see Foreword).

Maintenance

A canoe should be kept ashore and preferably under cover. If kept outside it is best inverted on supports, so that air may circulate inside. A sheet pegged over it will protect it almost as well as storing indoors (Fig. 20A).

Indoors racks may be arranged, preferably with crossbars about one-quarter of the length in from each end (Fig. 20B). If the canoe is stowed wet it may be inverted, otherwise it is better left open the right way up. A canoe may also hang by webbing straps from a roof (Fig. 20C).

A folding canoe stored assembled may distort. It depends for its shape on parts sprung to curves. If the framework is dismantled and the parts allowed to straighten the canoe will keep its shape longer. Rubber tends to perish with age, particularly on tight folds. Consequently it is best to keep the skin open if possible, otherwise it should be folded in a different way from time to time.

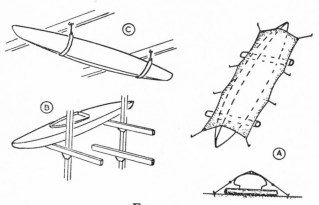

FIG. 20
Storing canoes

Washing out a rigid canoe is not advised, as this tends to deposit dirt at the inaccessible ends. Wiping mud with a damp cloth is better. A vacuum-cleaner will shift dry dirt. A blunt table knife will remove grit lodged under stringers. A canvas mat in the canoe will reduce maintenance work.

The outside of the canoe may be washed with warm water and detergent. Special preservatives are available for folding-canoe hulls. Touch up varnishwork to prevent water absorption. Repaint worn keel and bilge keels. Touch up paint on canvas, but do not overdo this painting, as too much will eventually crack. Proofed canvas decks may be revived with coloured proofing solution. A plastic surface should not need any treatment.

The surface of rubber and plastic materials will chafe, exposing the reinforced fabric and maybe causing rot. It is better to fit strips of material along stringers and other parts with adhesive, so that the strips take the wear and may be peeled off and replaced when damaged.

Bare patches on a wooden canoe should be touched up. If complete stripping is needed, a chemical stripper is

97

safer than a blow-lamp. Glassfibre needs no special maintenance, but where parts made of other materials are involved, appropriate storage precautions should be taken.

Repairs

Damage may not be frequent, but every canoe should carry a repair kit, which may be basically the same for most kinds of canoe, as emergency repairs to wood and glassfibre are most easily done with fabric.

The minimum contents of the kit should be a few yards of thread and a needle, some pieces of fabric and some suitable adhesive. Scissors are almost essential and cutting pliers are useful. Electrician's tape makes temporary repairs to woodwork. Pack the kit in its own waterproof bag.

The most frequent repair is the patching of a small cut (Plate 14). The skin must be dry and clean—methylated spirit will remove moisture. Paint should be rubbed down with glasspaper or scraped with a knife so as to expose fibres. A small cut may be patched directly, but if more than an inch long the edges should be pulled together first by stitching. Stout domestic thread may be used, although sail twine is better. A triangular sail needle, about gauge 17, goes with it.

The best stitch is a herringbone made with double thread (Fig. 21A). Make the stitches about $\frac{1}{4}$ in. apart. Patching material should be the same type as the skin, if possible, although a lighter grade will be easier to fix. Round all corners to reduce the risk of the patch curling back. Fraying the edge of a canvas patch serves the same purpose. For a rubberized skin it is possible to use prepared tyre repair patches.

For canvas, the usual adhesive is black reclaim cement, which is applied to both surfaces and allowed to dry before pressing together. For plastic, the special adhesive is quicker acting. For rubber, the reclaim cement may be used, or ordinary rubber solution is cleaner. Where damage

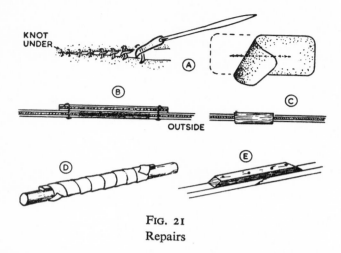

FIG. 21
Repairs

is alongside a wooden part, it is best to lift this so that the patch can go under it.

Damage to a wooden skin may be temporarily repaired with a canvas patch. Later, the damage must be cut out and a new piece fitted. In a plywood skin, one piece should fill the space and another inside support it. A few thin nails driven from outside and clenched inside may be needed (Fig. 21B). Very small damage may be squared up and filled with a solid block of wood, tapered slightly and pressed from inside (Fig. 21C). It is planed off after the glue has set.

A glassfibre hull is unlikely to be damaged, but if it is, a piece of fabric may be fixed temporarily. A permanent repair is made by filling the hole with resin, reinforced with glass-cloth if the damage is large, then sanding flush when hard.

Waterproof self-adhesive tapes are made and these may be used for temporarily patching most materials. They, and electrician's tape, may be used for binding a splint on broken wood (Fig. 21D). A permanent structural repair is made by glueing and screwing a reinforcing piece over the damage (Fig. 21E).

Sail and Power

A CANOEIST should always remember that his craft is designed for propulsion by paddle. Using other methods may work, but they may not be as successful as if used in a craft particularly designed for them. A paddling canoe under sail cannot be expected to have the same performance as a class sailing dinghy. Nor will it take an outboard motor like a proper motor-boat hull. However, if the prime purpose is always remembered and too much is not expected of the other methods of propulsion there is nothing wrong with adding to your interest by using them.

Sail

Many new canoeists consider adding sail after they have mastered their craft under paddles. Whether it is worth while depends on the canoe and on what is expected. The most efficient canoe under paddles is the least efficient under sail. Any canoe is too long in relation to its beam to be very efficient under sail, but a roomy two-seater, particularly if it is short, can have a reasonable performance. A 15 ft. two-seater with a beam of 32 in. can be rigged to sail fairly well, but a longer two-seater suffers from lack of manœuvrability, and a slim single-seater of any length will not be able to support a mast of sufficient height for the rig to be efficient. Most paddling touring canoes have straight keels. A boat built for sailing has its keel rockered—swept up towards the ends. This allows for quick turning. The great

length of straight keel of the average canoe makes any turns
to be of considerable radius unless a paddle is used.

Another snag with adding sails to a canoe is the difficulty
of getting the sail plan balanced in relation to the hull without interfering with accommodation. The only satisfactory
place for the mast is at or near the point of the cockpit. A
small sail plan on this mast will have its centre of effort
too far forward and it will be impossible to turn the canoe
up into the wind. This is a dangerous arrangement, as it
means that the canoe will sail in the direction the wind is
going, but not more than a few degrees each side of that.
The correct way to stop a sailing-boat is to turn it up
into the wind. If the boat will not turn up into the
wind it cannot be stopped, except by lowering the sail.
Many sails offered with canoes have this fault. Providing
the owner knows they can only be used for running
they may be acceptable, but they are no use for serious
sailing.

A canoe as used for paddling has a very shallow draught
and if attempts are made to sail in any direction except
downwind it will make so much leeway as to be no use. To
prevent this blowing sideways some keel surface must be
provided. In a yacht there is a fixed keel. In a sailing dinghy
there is a centreboard. In a canoe a fixed keel would be
dangerous if it fouled the bottom and a centreboard case
would interfere with accommodation. The alternative is
a pair of leeboards, which provide keel area by hanging
down the sides, usually fixed to a crossbar over the cockpit
coaming. This is satisfactory, and is also seen on many
Dutch yachts and on Thames sailing barges. A deep rudder
also serves to prevent leeway, as well as provide the means
of steering.

If a sail is only wanted to take advantage of the wind
when it is blowing in the way you wish to go, quite a simple
rig may be carried. As there is no problem of leeway,
leeboards are not needed, and steering may be by a paddle
trailed over the side. The sail may be almost any shape for

this type of sailing, and a balanced lug is often chosen (Fig. 22A). The mast fits at the point of the cockpit. The yard is hoisted by a halliard through a screw-eye and the end of the boom is hauled back to the mast by a tack line. As the boat can only be stopped by lowering the sail, it is best to bring the end of the halliard back to a cleat within reach, if sailing single-handed.

Two devices are used to bring the centre of effort of the sail plan far enough back in relation to the hull. There may be a foresail or jib as well as a mainsail, when a mizzen mast is stepped behind the cockpit and the combination of the sail area on this mast with the other two sails balances the plan (Fig. 22B). This ketch rig appeals to some people, but it is only satisfactory when there is plenty of room—there are too many things to look after for sailing to be efficient or pleasant in narrow waters, where changes of direction are frequent. The mizzen sheet passes through an eye on the stern and is brought forward to a cleat on the coaming. The rear person tends this and holds the main sheet in his hand while steering with his feet. The forward person deals with the leeboards and handles the jib sheets.

It is more efficient and less trouble to have most of the sail area in the mainsail, with a small jib and no mizzen sail. This is only possible if the canoe has sufficient beam to support a reasonable height of mast. The sail for this purpose is a gunter, in which the gaff continues vertically above the top of the mast. (Fig. 22C). The mast is held by a forestay and two shrouds to the gunwales. If it stands on a little thwart across the coaming sides and the shrouds have guyline runners (Fig. 22D), in an emergency the whole rig can be dropped overboard by releasing a slide, instead of the crew going in. The boom is made long enough to bring the centre of the plan well aft. A canoe with this rig can be sailed with the forward man almost laying down, to act as ballast, while the helmsman sits up on a side deck if necessary, and steers with a fore-and-aft tiller (Fig. 22E). For a paddling canoe this is the rig most likely to give

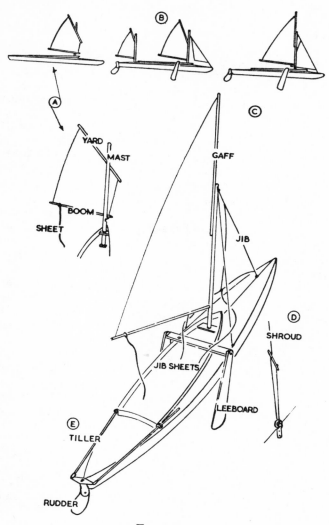

FIG. 22
Sailing gear

satisfactory sailing, particularly if it is beamy in relation to
its length.

Around the turn of this century, when canoes were
developing away from paddling into sailing machines, some
very fast sailing craft were designed which were no use at
all under paddles. From these have come the International
10 square metre Sailing Canoes, which until the recent
development of racing catamarans were the fastest sailing
machines in the world. The hull is between 16 ft. 0 in. and
17 ft. 0¾ in. long, and between 3 ft. 1⅜in. and 3 ft. 7¼ in. beam.
It is decked completely, so as to make a watertight box into
which the centreboard and rudder fit through trunks. The
sail area is 10 square metres (107·64 square feet) in a jib and
a Bermudan main sail. The helmsman spends most of his
time on a sliding seat balancing the boat. Capsizes are
expected and the helmsman is able to right the boat himself
by standing on the centreboard and levering on the sliding
seat, so that he may climb on board and sail on.

Compared with the number of sailing dinghies there have
never been many international sailing canoes, but they
enjoy a unique prestige. In Britain these canoes are sailed
by the Royal Canoe Club. The Sailing Challenge Cup has
been competed for annually since 1874 except for war years.
The International Cup, offered by the New York Canoe
Club in 1886, is competed for by challenge. In 1959 the
cup was brought to Britain by Bill Kempner and Alan Emus,
after a decisive win in three races. Since 1933, when Britain
won, the Americans challenged unsuccessfully in 1936 and
1948, then succeeded in 1952. A British challenge was un-
successful in 1953.

Beside these International sailing canoes, other first-class
sailing canoes sail as a 'B' class. The 'C' class was a type of
cheap canvas-covered sailing canoe devised by the Clyde
Canoe Club and sailed mainly on Loch Lomond, but few of
these craft are now in use.

The canoeist may consider joining two canoes to make a
sailing catamaran, in the hope of achieving a performance

comparable with specially built catamarans. This is unlikely to be successful. The hulls of a catamaran have a very different form. Many special catamarans are difficult to make go about when tacking and an improvisation based on two canoes is likely to be less effective. Hull spacing, the location and size of centreboards, the arrangement of rudders, and the design of the sail plan are all more critical than for single-hulled craft. Joining two canoe hulls may provide some fun, but too high a performance should not be expected.

Of course, the technique of sailing is much the same whatever the craft. There is no room in a book of this size for instructions on sailing; the reader with an urge to sail should obtain one of the many excellent books on sailing, such as *Tackle Sailing*.[1]

Power

To some purists the idea of driving a canoe with a motor is unthinkable, but small power units are accepted for many things and the canoeist who uses a motor is following a trend and joining the growing fraternity of small-power-boat men. Power may become more acceptable as years pass by. A canoe has very easy lines and it is surprising how little power is needed to propel it. One canoe sideboard motor which can drive a canoe as fast as two paddlers, and keep it up all day, is only $\frac{1}{3}$ h.p. and can run for about eighteen hours on a gallon of petrol, which is a contrast to the petrol-thirsty outboard motors of the high-speed runabout enthusiast.

An outboard motor cannot be located at the stern, as it would be out of reach, although some Canadian canoes have been built with cut-off sterns so as to provide a transom for the motor within reach of the helmsman. It is more usual to mount the motor at one side, which is not such an unbalanced arrangement as might be expected. The thrust from the propeller keeps the canoe on an even keel.

[1] Published by Stanley Paul & Co.

In general an outboard motor mounted at the side is unsatisfactory on a single-seater as trimming the boat for proper steering is difficult. On a two-seater of normal proportions the set-up is satisfactory.

A fairly substantial crossbar is needed to resist torque. This may be wood, or a metal tube is better for some motors. It may be fixed by hook bolts to the coaming or bolted through a reinforcing block under the deck. As the 'passing port to port' rule means that a canoe is more likely to come closer to the right bank than the left, the motor is best kept from the risk of touching the bottom by mounting on the port side. However, this is not very important. The extension of the crossbar should keep the motor reasonably close.

A normal small outboard motor intended for a dinghy may be used. The problem may be in finding one small enough—the power should be less than 1 h.p. If the height is adjustable it should be arranged so that the propeller is only a few inches below the surface, providing this does not bring the power-head too high. A sideboard motor differs in having the propeller shaft straight out of the power head (Fig. 23). This brings the propeller farther aft and reduces the tendency to turn the canoe.

With a power unit on the side steering has to be done by a rudder. If the motor is designed to swivel, it must be

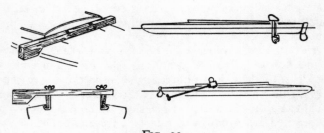

FIG. 23
Outboard-motor fittings

locked in the ahead position. A foot-operated rudder is best, as the motor can be attended to without letting go of the steering arrangements. It is possible to experiment with the angle of the motor so that it can be arranged to thrust inwards slightly and counteract its tendency to turn the canoe by its off-centre position.

An outboard motor has been mounted centrally through the bottom of a specially adapted canoe, and the English Channel has been crossed with this arrangement. Electric power has been tried, but the snag is the weight of the batteries. A canoe may be driven silently using a car-starter motor connected to a propeller at the end of a flexible shaft, held over the side, but the size of the battery limits this to being a novelty for a brief period. On the Thames there are large electric canoes equipped for plugging into the mains for charging over night.

Other methods

To the paddling enthusiast the idea of rowing a canoe is even more unthinkable than using a motor on it, but it has been done. Looked at scientifically, rowing is more mechanically efficient than paddling—you get more for the same amount of effort. Canadian canoes have been equipped with out-riggers carrying rowlocks, and sliding seats installed in the hull, to make a fast rowing boat. A duck punt is not far removed from a decked canoe, and that is normally rowed.

Canadian canoes have been poled as a sport in the same way as punting. This is a very specialized activity, but four men who know what they are doing can make a large canoe move. In Canada and the U.S.A. poling is often used to get canoes up rapids and to steady them when going down. Poling should not be impossible in a large-decked canoe.

On a narrow waterway, such as a canal, when there is a strong headwind, it is easier to tow from the bank than to attempt to paddle against it. The towline should be as long as possible. This makes steering the canoe easier. The best point to tow from is not the bow, but somewhere about the point of the cockpit. In a two-seater, where one person tows and the other steers with a paddle over the side, the exact towing point is not important, but it is possible to find a point where the canoe will keep straight even when no one is on board.

Appendix 1

BIBLIOGRAPHY

Other relevant books by Percy W. Blandford:

Canoeing (Foyle)
Boat Building (Foyle)
Canoes and Canoeing (Lutterworth)
Canoeing Waters (Lutterworth)
Scouts on the Water (Scout Association)
The Art of Sailing (Evans)

MODERN BOOKS

These publications are a selection from those known to the author, and are suggested as worth-while reading for anyone wishing to learn more about the many aspects of canoeing. All are either in print or recently out of print, and deal with canoeing as practised today.

Boating. Educational Productions. Booklet
Book of Canoeing. A. Ellis (Brown, Son & Ferguson). General
Canoeing. American Red Cross. Canadian canoes
Canoeing. Luscombe and Bird (Black). General
Cockleshell Heroes. Lucas Phillips (Pan). War exploits
Eskimo Roll. British Canoe Union. One of several booklets
Guide to Canoeing. London Federation of Boys' Clubs. Booklet
Kayak to Cape Wrath. J. L. Henderson (McLellan). W. Scotland
Starting Canoeing. M. Russell (Coles). Introductory
The Canoeing Manual. N. McNaught (Kaye). General
You and Your Canoe. O. J. Cock (Benn). General

OLDER BOOKS

These books are out of print, but may be obtainable secondhand or from libraries, and contain useful information as well as things of historical interest.

1000 miles in the 'Rob Roy' canoe
The 'Rob Roy' on the Baltic
The 'Rob Roy' on the Jordan
    John McGregor. (The pioneer story)

Canoeing
The Heart of England by Waterway
Rapid Rivers
    William Bliss. (Classics of canoeing. Much waterway information)

Canoe Errant
Canoe Errant on the Nile
Canoe Errant on the Mississippi
Canoe to Mandalay
Canoe to Australia
    R. Raven-Hart. (Probably the most-travelled canoeist)

An Inland Voyage. Robert Louis Stevenson. (Literature)
Canoe Travelling. W. Baden-Powell. (Sailing in Baltic)
The Heart of Scotland by Waterway. R. A. Downie (Touring)
Water Music. Sir John Squire (Trip with Wm. Bliss).

TOURING INFORMATION

The canoe-touring information generally available is not as comprehensive as may be desired, but greater details can be obtained through clubs.

MAPS

Canoeing map of England and Wales
Inland cruising map of England
River Thames, Richmond to Lechlade
Norfolk Broads
Rivers Medway and Swale
Essex Rivers
Yachtsman's coastal charts
    Edward Stanford

Yachtsman's coastal charts. Imray, Laurie, Norie & Wilson
British Waterways—canal system. British Waterways
Fenland Waterways. Appleyard Lincoln
Rivers Severn and Avon. Alun Jones
Great Ouse and tributaries. Great Ouse Boating Association
Chichester Harbour. Bosun's Locker
River Wye. P. W. Blandford

BOOKS

Guide to Waterways of British Isles. British Canoe Union
(Itineraries)
Inland Waterways. Imray, Laurie, Norie & Wilson (For larger
craft)
Nicholson's Guides to the Waterways (four books—David &
Charles)
Getting Afloat. Link House (Launching sites)

PERIODICALS

Many outdoor and yachting magazines carry occasional canoeing articles, but these are of particular interest:

Small Boat. Link House Publications (Monthly)
Canoe-Camper. Canoe-Camping Club (Quarterly)
Canoeing in Britain. British Canoe Union (Quarterly)
White Water. Through clubs (Quarterly)
American White Water. Through clubs (Quarterly)

NAUTICAL BOOKS

These books are suggested as good guides to subjects related to
canoeing:

Starting to Sail. Fisher (Coles). Introductory
Tackle Sailing. Dawson (Stanley Paul). Comprehensive
Complete Amateur Boat Building. Verney (Murray). All
methods

The Boatman's Manual. Lane (Norton, USA). Basic seamanship

A Beginner's Guide to the Sea. Knight (Macmillan). Basic seamanship

Coastal Navigation Wrinkles. Rantzen (Coles). Finding your way

Make Your Own Sails. Bowker and Budd (Macmillan)

Knots and Splices. Day (Coles). Essential knotting

Small Boat Navigation. Hepherd (Stanley Paul). Basic navigation.

Appendix 2

Many organizations, particularly those concerned with training young people, have adopted safety codes. The following points summarize the main items and the author believes they form a reasonable guide for any canoeist. A compromise has to be made between being too safety conscious and stifling any spirit of adventure, and relaxing rules to the stage where a beginner may unknowingly get himself into a dangerous situation.

1. Be able to swim a reasonable distance before using a canoe on water over wading depth.

2. Wear a lifejacket in dangerous rapids and at sea.

3. Provide the canoe with reserve buoyancy.

4. Never wear rubber boots or heavy clothing.

5. Never leave a capsized canoe, and do not attempt to right it if it can be got to the bank.

6. Keep away from weirs, both above and below.

7. Keep out of the way of other craft.

8. Never tackle a waterway without first getting information on it and always inspect hazards before tackling them.

9. Never tackle hazardous waters alone, and tell others where you are going when you leave on a lengthy trip.

Appendix 3

CANOE–CAMPING KIT

Every camper has his own ideas about equipment, but this list is offered as a guide or check list when planning a canoe-camping holiday. As a group of four has been found to be the most convenient unit for sharing gear and cooking, quantities are given for four. The type of tour will affect what is taken—a trip remote from habitations and suppliers will have to be more fully equipped than one passing through thickly populated areas. The duration of the trip and the type of water also affect what should be taken.

Essential items	*Optional items*
CRAFT	
2 double, or 4 single, canoes, with spray covers, buoyancy bags, paddles and painters. 1 repair kit and 2 sponges	Spare paddle Sailing gear Trolley
CLOTHING	
Each person: shirt, shorts, underwear and sweater. Shore-going clothes. Waterproof jacket or anorak. Sandals or plimsols. Emergency clothing and towel in waterproof bag.	Rain coat Swimming costume Sun glasses Jack knife Lifejacket
SLEEPING	
2 tents with poles and groundsheets 4 sleeping bags Pyjamas	2 flysheets 4 sheet linings Air beds Candle lamps Torches

Essential Items	*Optional items*

EATING

2 pressure or gas stoves

2 canteens, or one frypan and 3 billy-cans

4 water bottles

4 each: knife, fork, large and small spoons

8 plates, plastic or enamel, some deep

4 mugs

1 tin opener

Matches in bottle

Fuel containers or spare gas cartridges

4 wiping-up cloths

Optional: Spare stove, Plastic bowl, Plastic folding bucket, Bread knife, Egg slice, Dish mop, Pressure cooker, Steel wool, Detergent, Stove windscreen

PERSONAL

Each person: towel, soap, comb, handkerchiefs, toothbrush, etc.

1 clothes repair kit

1 first-aid kit

Maps and itineraries

Optional: Mirror, Toilet roll, Trowel, Cameras, Compass

PACKAGES

4 fully waterproof kitbags

Other containers for cooking gear

Plastic and metal pots and containers for food

Optional: More waterproof bags

Appendix 4

GLOSSARY

NOTE: Those items marked 'S' are only applicable to sailing.

Aft: Towards the stern.

Anorak, Anarak: A canoeing coat, without front opening and usually with a hood.

Auxiliary deck: Alternative name for spray cover.

Bailer: A scoop for removing water from the inside of a boat—a sponge is more useful in a canoe.

Belay: Make fast, by tying a rope to something.

Bight: The loop of a doubled rope.

Board (S): One leg of the sailing course when tacking to windward.

Boil: In fast water, an upsurge of water causing a mound above the surface.

Bolt rope (S): The rope sewn around the edge of the sail.

Bottom boards: Removable flooring in any craft.

Bow: The forward part of a boat.

Bunt (S): Middle part of a sail.

Cable: The rope or line used on an anchor.

Carry away: Break or collapse.

Carvel: A method of planking, using strips laid fore and aft, flush with each other.

Centreboard (S): A keel which hinges up into a watertight case.

Chine: The angle between the side and the bottom in some types of hull.

Chute: A narrow clear channel through a rapid.

Clinker: A method of planking, using strips fore and aft, lapped over each other.

Close-hauled (S): Sailing at as close an angle to the wind as possible.

Coaming: The board around the edge of the cockpit.

Cockpit: The part of the craft in which the crew sit in a decked canoe.

Cringle (S): A thimble, or loop, worked into the edge of a sail.

Dagger board (S): A keel which can be raised and lowered by moving it up and down through a watertight box.

Deck: The protective top covering of a closed canoe.

Double chine: A hull with two chines at each side.

Double diagonal: A method of planking using two skins of planks laid diagonally to the keel and crossing each other.

Draw stroke: Stroke used to pull the canoe sideways.

Drip rings: Rings fitted round the neck of double-bladed paddles to break the flow of water running down the shaft from the raised blade.

Ease away (S): Slacken the sheet of a sail.

Eddy: Where the current turns back on itself due to an obstruction or the shape of the bank or bed.

Ensign: The national flag, flown at the stern.

Eskimo kayak: A slender-decked craft, with a small cockpit and unswept stem.

Eskimo roll: A complete turn over, under the water at one side and up the other.

Fairlead: A guide for a rope.

Fall: Loose hanging end of rope.

Feather: The paddle blade above the water and parallel to it.

Ferry glide: A method of using the current to cause the canoe to cross the main flow.

Foresail (S): The triangular sail forward of the mast, often called a jib.

Freeboard: The height of the gunwale above the waterline.

Gate: One of the obstacles on a slalom course, usually consisting of hanging poles.

Go about (S): Change tack against the wind.

Graveyard: Boulder-choked river-bed, in fast water.

Gripe: Tend to fly up into the wind.

Gunwale: The upper edge of the hull.

Gybe (S): Change tack by turning away from the wind.

Hard chine: A hull with an angle between the side and the bottom.

Haystack: A standing wave caused by fast water hitting slower water.

Heave-to (S): Bring the boat head to wind.

Hog: The central internal lengthwise member of a hull above the keel.

Hogged: The hull sagging towards the ends.

Irons (S): Head to wind with the sails flapping loose.

J stroke: Paddling with a single-bladed paddle so as to steer at the end of each stroke.

Jib (S): A triangular sail forward of the mast.

Kayak, kyak: Originally the Eskimo craft, but sometimes applied to any rigid-decked canoe.

Keel: The central outside member of a hull.

Keelson: A central lengthwise structural member above the keel, sometimes applied to the part of a canoe which is more correctly called a hog.

Ketch (S): Rig with two masts, having main and fore sails on the forward mast, and another sail on the mizzen mast, stepped forward of the rudder post.

Leeboards (S): Boards hanging at the side of a boat to take the place of a keel in preventing leeway.

Leeward: Away from the wind (pronounced 'looard').

Leeway: Drifting sideways from the wind.

Lock: A kind of water lift, used for moving a boat from one water level to another.

Luff (S): To sail nearer the wind.

Main sail (S): The sail aft of the largest mast.

Mizzen sail (S): The sail aft of the rear mast on a yawl or ketch.

Moulded plywood: Hull built from veneers glued diagonally in several layers.

Paddle (*Lock*): Sluice for emptying and filling a lock.

Painter: The rope attached to bow or stern.

Pawlata: A method of Eskimo rolling, with a technique between the put-across and the screw.

Pennant, pendant: A triangular flag, usually denoting club.

Port: The left side, facing forward.

Pound: A section of canal between locks.

Push-over: Paddle stroke used to move the canoe sideways.

Put across: The basis method of Eskimo rolling.

Rapid: General term for a stretch of fast rough water.

Reach: A section of river between locks or hazards.

Reach (S): Sail at right angles to the wind.

Ready-about (S): The order indicating a change of tack.

Riffle: A small shallow rapid.

Rock garden: Similar to graveyard, but in easier water.

Rocker: Keel curved up towards the ends.

Round bottomed: A hull with rounded cross-sections.

Run (S): Sail before the wind.

Run off: Additional water in a river due to rain or melting snow.

Screw: A method of Eskimo rolling. Most difficult but most useful, as the hands remain in the normal paddling position.

Scull: Use the paddle blade diagonal to the water in alternate directions.

Seam batten: Method of planking similar to carvel, but with each seam covered by a batten.

Sharpie: A V-bottom type of hull.

Sheet (S): The rope controlling a sail.

Shoal: Shallow water.

Slalom: A contest in which obstacles have to be negotiated in a section of fast water.

Sloop (S): A one-mast rig having a main sail and one fore sail.

Sluice: A water-controlling gate which can be adjusted with a handle (windlass) for regulating the flow of water past lock gates or weirs. Called a 'paddle' on some waterways.

Snag: A branch or other obstruction lodged in the river-bed.

Spray cover: A form of apron fitting over the cockpit coaming and around the canoeist.

Squaw stroke: Alternative name for J stroke.

Starboard: Right-hand side when facing forward.

Stem: The upright member at the forward point of a canoe.

Stern: The rear of the canoe.

Sternpost: The upright member at the stern.

Stopper: A large wave in a rapid or below a weir, of sufficient size to stop or capsize a canoe.

Stringer: Lengthwise member of a canoe framework.

Tack (S): Sail a zig-zag course so that the wind comes from alternate sides.

Tack, port (S): Tack with the wind on the port side.

Tack, starboard (S): Tack with the wind on the starboard side.

Telemark: A method of turning quickly by leaning inwards and taking the weight with the paddle extended.

Thimble: A metal ring, round which a rope is spliced.

Throw: Stroke similar to push-over, used by bowman in a Canadian canoe.

Thwart: Seat or other member fitted across the hull.

Trim: The level of a boat.

Una (S): Any sailing rig with a single sail.

Underwater stroke: Returning the paddle edgewise without withdrawing it from the water.

Veer: Change direction.

Washboard: Name sometimes incorrectly given to coaming.

Weather helm (S): Tendency for craft to turn into the wind.

Weir: Where the water falls over an edge.

Whirlpool: Spinning water caused by opposing currents.

White water: Fast and turbulent water.

Windlass: On some waterways, the handle used to operate sluices.

Windward: Towards the wind.

Yaw: Swing from side to side.

Yawl (S): A sailing rig similar to a ketch, but with the mizzen mast stepped aft of the rudder post.

Yoke: The cross-piece on the head of a rudder, to which the controlling lines are attached.

Appendix 5

CANOEING WATERS

This book is intended to be a guide to how to canoe, not where to canoe—another book of the same size could be filled with waterways information. Details of suitable waters may be obtained from the sources mentioned in Appendix 1, but following is a list of selected rivers which may interest the reader. It is intended to provide no more than an indication of the character of the river and should not be acted on without further enquiries.

As rivers are affected in their character by differences in water level, the place named as the highest point may not always be a possible starting point. The total canoeing distance is approximate—in some cases there are dull stretches which may be omitted. The grading varies and is only given as a guide to the general character:

P. Placid and no serious hazards.
T. Tidal.

ROMAN NUMERALS. International rough-water grading.

In the availability column the position throughout the great part of the waterway is indicated:

F. Primarily a fishing river and may only be available out of season or by special permission.
R. A right of way.
X. Private, but canoeing is permitted if requested in advance, and usually on payment of a fee.
O. Not a right of way, but owners have not objected to canoes.

Main rivers are in alphabetical order. Tributaries are listed under the river they feed.

River	Highest point	Miles	Grade	Avail- ability
Arun	Stopham	25	T	R
— Rother	Midhurst	12	P	O
Avon, Bristol	Chippenham	38	P	O
Avon, Salisbury	Pewsey	70	P	F
Conway	Llanrwst	12	T	R
Dart	Totnes	11	T	R
Dee	Lake Bala	80	II-III	F
Eden	Kirkby Stephen	50	II-III	F
Essex rivers:				
— Blackwater	Maldon	10	T	R
— Colne	Castle Hedingham	20	T	R
— Crouch	Battlesbridge	15	T	R
— Roach	Stambridge Mills	4	T	R
Exe	Tiverton	25	II, T	O, R
Forth	Aberfoyle	37	P	F
Lune	Sedburgh	30	II	O
Nene	Northampton	60	P	X
Norfolk Broads:				
— Ant	Spa Common	13	P, T	X
— Bure	Aylsham	37	P, T	X
— Thurne	Hickling Broad	7	T	X
— Waveney	Diss	54	T	X
— Wensum	Ringland	12	P	O
— Yare	Norwich	39	T	X
Orwell	Stowmarket	28	P, T	R
Ouse, Great	Buckingham	140	P	O
— Cam	Hauxton Mill	33	P	O
— Ivel	Hitchin	20	P	O
— Lark	Bury St. Edmunds	12	P	O
— Little Ouse	Thetford	22	P	O
— Nar	Narborough	12	P	O
— Ouzel	Leighton Buzzard	15	P	O
— Wissey	Hilborough	25	P	O
Ouse, Yorks.	Linton Lock	46	P	R
— Nidd	Pateley Bridge	40	II-III	F
— Derwent	Ganton	55	P	R
— Swale	Richmond	50	II	F
— Wharfe	Kettlewell	70	II-IV	F
— Ure	Wensley	50	II-IV	F

| | | | | *Avail-* |
River	*Highest point*	*Miles*	*Grade*	*ability*
Severn	Welshpool	130	I-II	R
— Avon	Stratford	45	P	R
— Teme	Knighton	74	II	X
Spey	Newtonmore	73	I-III	F
Tamar	Wearde Quay	17	T	R
Tees	Middleton	69	III-IV	O
Teifi	Tregaron	55	III-IV	O
Thames	Lechlade	140	P, T	X
— Cherwell	Aynho	20	P	O
— Lee	Hertford	28	P	X
— Mole	Horley	45	P	O
— Wey	Farnham	35	P	O
Torridge	Hele Bridge	21	I	O
Trent	Rugeley	140	I, P, T	R
— Derwent	Hathersage	50	I	O
— Dove	Clifton Bridge	30	I	O
— Penk and Sow	Penkridge	12	P	O
— Soar	Leicester	25	P	X
Wye	Glasbury	100	I	R
— Lugg	Leominster	23	P	O
— Monnow	Monmouth Cap	19	II	O

Index